QUILT STUDIO

Tweed Reflections II (detail). See full quilt on page iii. Photo: Keith Tidball

INNOVATIVE TECHNIQUES FOR

CONFIDENT AND CREATIVE

QUILTMAKING AND DESIGN

QUILT STUDIO

Tweed Reflections II, 1995, 48" × 48" (121 cm × 121 cm). Photo: Keith Tidball

PAULINE BURBIDGE

THE QUILT DIGEST PRESS
NTC/Contemporary Publishing Group

Library of Congress Cataloging-in-Publication Data

Burbidge, Pauline.
    Quilt studio : innovative techniques for confident and creative quiltmaking and design / Pauline Burbidge.
        p.   cm.
    Includes bibliographical references and index.
    ISBN 0-8442-2082-5
    1. Patchwork.   2. Quilting.   3. Appliqué.   4. Dyes and dyeing.
Domestic.   5. Textile painting.   6. Quilts—Design.   I. Title.
    TT835.B815   2000
    746.46—dc21
                                                                99-43585
                                                                CIP

Editorial and production direction by Anne Knudsen
Art direction by Kim Bartko
Project editing by Heidi Bresnahan
Book design by Hespenheide Design
Cover design by Kim Bartko
Front-cover photo and author photo by Keith Tidball
Back-cover photo by John Coles
Drawings by Kandy Petersen
Photography by Keith Tidball, unless otherwise indicated
Manufacturing direction by Pat Martin

Published by The Quilt Digest Press
A division of NTC/Contemporary Publishing Group, Inc.
4255 West Touhy Avenue, Lincolnwood (Chicago), Illinois 60712-1975, U.S.A.
Copyright © 2000 by Pauline Burbidge
Printed and bound in Hong Kong by Midas Printing, Inc.
International Standard Book Number: 0-8442-2082-5
25 24 23 22 21 20 19 18 17 16 15 14 13 12 11 10 9 8 7 6 5 4 3 2 1

Quilt Studio is dedicated to my husband, Charlie, to say thank you for helping me go through the lengthy process of completing the book.

Special thanks also to Michele Walker, Penny McMorris, and Keith Tidball for their valued help and contributions.

Contents

Flower Pot (detail). See full quilt on page 107. Photo: John Coles, Cornwall

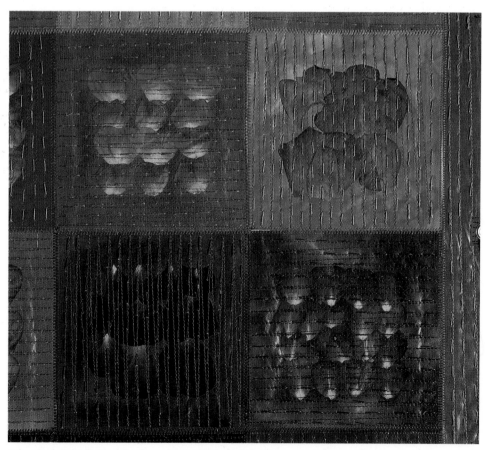

Colour Study I (detail). See full quilt on page 64. Photo: Keith Tidball

Author's Preface

When I first began quiltmaking in 1975, I had a very strong feeling that this was a turning point in my life. That has turned out to be so. My love of color, texture, and fabric drew me to quilts, but it was my earlier training in art and design that first helped me appreciate the beauty of traditional patchwork.

As you browse through my book, you may at first feel that the imagery I use is not traditional. Yet as you look more closely and as you learn more about the techniques I use, you will see that my work is inspired by patchwork traditions. The block-style quilts I made when I first began quiltmaking and the fabric collage that I have most recently discovered are in many ways similar.

I think of myself as a quiltmaker, craftsperson, designer, and textile artist, and I think my quilts reflect this. I like to think of my work as continuously changing and growing in the same way that nature does. Without change, it would become lifeless. I want the design projects in my book to inspire you to enjoy a similar love of color, texture, and fabric, opening opportunities for change and development in your own work.

Pauline Burbidge in her studio.
Photo: Keith Tidball

The book is structured into a series of Workshops. Each Workshop offers projects that help you practice and build confidence in your quiltmaking. Each also reflects my own development as a quiltmaker and my approach to teaching others. In *Quilt Studio*, I encourage you to use the projects as tools to develop your own themes and your own style, rather than teach you how to make specific quilts or follow patterns. It is your interpretation of each project that is important, for this is what will make the quilts you create unique.

The Workshops in Part One cover technique. They are designed so that a complete beginner can pick up the book, run through each project, and learn all essential quiltmaking skills from scratch. Experienced quilters can skip through this part of the book fairly rapidly, selecting only those techniques that are least familiar or that offer fresh ideas or approaches to familiar tasks.

The Workshops in Part Two explore the design process. This section of the book is also built around specific projects. The objective is to help you gain confidence as you try out different approaches to designing quilts, overcoming the mental barriers that too often stifle creativity. As you work through the projects you will find that they will spark thoughts and ideas that you can easily develop into designs of your own.

I hope that *Quilt Studio* will be enjoyed by quiltmakers, textile enthusiasts, and others worldwide who are interested in art and design. Whether quilting is the first creative outlet you have explored or whether you are coming to it from another creative field, it is my hope that my book will both instruct and inspire you. For me, there is no experience as exciting as watching ideas transform into fabric. It is my wish that this book will help you discover new avenues in design, which allow you to experience some of the special moments that go with being creative.

Pauline Burbidge

Chequered Cube (detail). See full quilt on page 84.

Introduction

by Michele Walker

Pauline Burbidge began making pieced quilts in the mid-1970s and was part of a new generation of artists who chose to work in the craft. Common to most quiltmakers, she did not come from a quilting background and is self-taught. She studied fashion and textiles at St. Martin's School of Art, London. This was followed by the establishing of her own company for which she designed clothes. Her skills as a pattern cutter have always been evident in her quiltmaking. The ability to visualize an image into sewable units, together with her instinctive design ability and use of color, were qualities that from the beginning were to place her in the forefront of quiltmakers both in Britain and in the United States.

QUILTMAKING REVIVAL

Financially, Pauline did not choose an easy career and is one of the few professional quiltmakers in her own country. British quilts until recently have not had the same respect and documentation that their American counterparts have received. There are few commissions and collectors in the private sector, and work is purchased mainly through museums and public art galleries. During the 1920s and '30s, crafts such as weaving, ceramics, and printed textiles underwent a creative revival. However, quiltmaking remained firmly in the traditional mold and was still regarded as a utilitarian craft with emphasis on traditional patterns and skills. It was thought of as "old-fashioned,"

Pauline Burbidge in her studio, 1979

and even in the early 1970s a large London exhibition showed predominantly hexagon designs, hand sewn with backing papers. Patchwork and quilting were frequently regarded as two separate techniques not necessarily used together on the same quilt.

Pauline was at art school during the years 1968 to '73, and it was at this time that crafts once more became popular. At the time she was living close to London's Portobello Road, an area renowned for antiques and flea markets. She had access to and was familiar with period textiles, clothes, and secondhand books. It was the discovery of a small book called *Old Patchwork Quilts and the Women Who Made Them*, by Ruth Finley, written in 1929, that inspired the making of her first quilt. The chance finding of

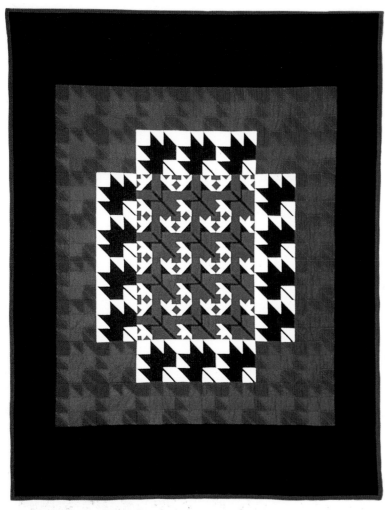

Day Lily, 1976, 83″ × 104″ (210 cm × 264 cm). Photo: Pauline Burbidge

that book came at a significant time in her career. Pauline felt jaded working in the fashion industry and wanted to use fabric and color in a "purer way." Although she describes her first quilt as "very ordinary," she instinctively knew she had found her métier.

EARLY QUILTS

Pauline was immediately drawn to the pieced quilts that used geometric shapes and straight seams. She then discovered Amish quilts and was fascinated by the unusual use of color and plain fabrics; also the integration of the quilting and patchwork patterns. These elements laid the foundation of her career. *Day Lily*, a quilt that combined two different blocks, immediately showed a bold, graphic approach. The repeated block was to remain a constant in Pauline's work, as it gave her the design flexibility that she required. From the beginning she chose to sew by machine and devised a method that allowed the quilting stitch to sink out of sight in the seam line. As with many makers who began at the time— Michael James and myself, for example— working on traditional type quilts served as an apprenticeship to the subject. It is difficult to imagine today, with the phenomenal amount of classes, books, fabrics, and gadgets on offer, how little information was available. One learned by trial and error and in isolation. Due to the nonexistence of suitable plain-colored fabrics, Pauline also became a skilled dyer.

She soon began designing her own quilts and devised a strip technique for a series on pieced pictures, 1976 to 1980. The image was simplified to a geometric shape that was divided into strips for easy piecing. Each strip was in one piece until a color change, which necessitated a seam, as shown in *Heron* on page 56. The use of strips and the color black were to be a constant feature of her work to the present day. Many of her early figurative quilts reflected bric-a-brac that had caught her eye in the stalls on Portobello Road. The *Flying Ducks* series was inspired by a dust jacket from a book.

From the mid-1970s in Britain, interest in quiltmaking was gaining momentum. The renowned exhibition "American Pieced Quilts" toured Europe and visited London in 1973 to '74. An American quilt collector, Joan Zinni, also opened a shop and held exhibitions and classes. This venue acted as a catalyst for quilt enthusiasts and lasting friendships were made. At this time the American influence overshadowed the British tradition, and the revival was well underway with Pauline Burbidge established as the most innovative maker.

CHANGE OF DIRECTION

A hallmark of Pauline's work is her meticulous attention to detail and technique. In her early work, prior to the quiltmaking, a colored design was precisely executed on graph paper. This was an approach common to many quiltmakers during that early period and was frequently taught in workshops. As Pauline began working on commission, these renderings were valuable to clients eager to see an illustration of the final piece. Pauline's emphasis has always been on the design, which can be a lengthy and intense process that takes weeks rather than days. For a commission based on Egyptian art, she spent many hours drawing in the galleries of the British Museum.

Throughout her career Pauline has constantly sought new challenges. By 1980, feeling that her work needed a change of direction she looked again at traditional patterns, selecting those that gave a three-dimensional illusion. She was intrigued by pattern and the different effects that occurred when a unit was repeated, but also felt it necessary to find a fresh approach, to break away from the symmetry of historical work. An early piece in this new series was *Cubic Log Cabin*, 1982 (see page 77). The design was based on two well-known patterns, *Tumbling Blocks* and *Log Cabin* that, by change of color and tone, twist and turn diagonally across the surface. The blocks underwent a metamorphosis from flat to illusory three-dimensional shapes. This style was to be recurrent to the present day. Pauline did a number of quilts in this three-dimensional geometric series that used traditional patterns in a new, innovative way. The series manifested itself in two large masterpieces, *Liquorice Allsorts* and *Mirrored Steps*, 1983 (see pages 72 and 85). Both suggest an architectural source, but they were in fact based on a cardboard model of steps with a mirror set at right angles on each side. This resulted in a series of reflected images, a more sophisticated version of her early kaleidoscope designs.

Ducks, 1978, 40″ × 40″ (102 cm × 102 cm). Photo: Pauline Burbidge

In 1982 Pauline received the John Ruskin Award (administered by the Crafts Council), which enabled her to produce new work toward an exhibition. She said in the catalog, "Although I have been making quilts for nearly eight years, I still feel very excited by the potential of this medium and feel that this work is just the tip of the iceberg." Her work also appeared in the prestigious Quilt National competition/exhibition for the first time and received an Award of Excellence. In 1983 she was invited by Michael James to participate in "Fabric Constructions—the Art Quilt," Massachusetts.

FREEDOM FROM RESTRICTIONS

Up to this point, Pauline's work, like that of most of her fellow exhibitors, was highly finished. The raw edges were neatly turned under and fabric pressed flat, denying its tactility. The work appeared disciplined and professional, but among the quiltmakers there was a growing dissatisfaction. The technical perfection was felt to be stultifying by those who sought a more responsive approach. It appeared to be the work of American quiltmaker Therese May that unshackled the contemporary quilt from this obsession. In 1985 her piece called *Sawblade* was in Quilt National and with its loose threads and raw edges set a different standard of acceptability. Ideas and rules of excellence were turned upside down. Pauline admired this new work, as she also felt restricted by the working process and was drawn to the spontaneity of the students she was teaching at the time. A desire to tune in with the flexibility of fabric and rhythms of stitch led her to look again at figurative subjects and in particular still life.

Ever mindful of the need to earn money, Pauline was now renting a studio in the Lace Market, Nottingham. She looked to other ways of speeding up her work production. In 1986, as part of an artist's placement scheme she worked in a commercial quilting factory. Having diligently learned how to thread and operate the machines, she agreed to rent one for a week each year. Although it gave her work a uniformity—the quilting stitch appeared predominantly on the surface—she was able to complete fifteen instead of two or three quilts. This gave her more time in which to develop a new style through her paper and fabric collage work. The new work still used an underlying grid but she began working in a way that acknowledged her experience as an artist. Her drawing ability came into its own. With years of experience and recognition behind her, this gave confidence to leap into fabric collage in which she created even wider boundaries for the contemporary quiltmaker. I have described her at this stage as "combining the freedom of a painter with the eye of a designer and the skill of a master craftsperson."

Her subject matter ranged from a series inspired by ships and docklands as part of a school residency—*Lowestoft*, 1987 (see page 99), and *Ship Shape*, 1989, for example—to domestic subjects like *Kate's Vase*, 1987 (see page 16), using a still life that was set up in the studio. In this work the blocks do not make such a regular grid as before and show Pauline's delight in multi-patterned layers and stripes. The movement from top left to bottom right is now a constant visual theme and hallmark of her quilts. As this new series progressed, so her working methods became freer. Besides making observational drawings she photographed images which were then transferred to paper collage. These were used as reference for the final quilt. At that point "drawing with scissors and fabric" aptly described her technique. Eventually, the rigidity of the industrial quilting pattern was at odds with the freedom of fabric collage. She gradually returned to using a domestic sewing machine and also "scribbled" across the surface with hand stitching.

A lecture tour to Australia in 1988 introduced Pauline to tropical fish and the moving rhythms of water. Inspired by a book titled *Coral Gardens* by Leni Riefenstahl, she began a new series based on fish and stripes. In *Joining Forces*, 1989 (see page 19), now hanging in the Whitworth Art Gallery, Manchester, two large fish shapes glide and merge Escher-like from opposite directions. The eye is once again deceived by the illusion. This is also experienced with the quilt called *Intercut Fish—Harmony*, 1991 (see page 86), where fishy shapes are camouflaged among the flickering waves that eddy across the surface.

Pauline's work on display in her kitchen and living room, Allanbank. Photo: Keith Tidball

At this point Pauline was still living in Nottingham, a city with canals and red brick warehouses which are relics of a past thriving textile industry. Before she left in 1993, still fascinated with water and reflections, Pauline made a visual record which later inspired several quilts, notably *Nottingham Reflections*, 1994 (see page 108), commissioned by Jack Walsh. This was the first quilt to be made in her new studio.

RECENT WORKS

When Pauline and her husband, sculptor Charles Poulsen, moved to a very different environment in the Scottish Borders, their first priority was the major one of converting a series of farm buildings into suitable working and living space. They approached it with the same discipline, commitment, and attention to detail as they do their own work, and a year later Pauline was working in her new studio overlooking the open fields and the meandering Blackadder and Whiteadder rivers. Her latest work is based on observation of her immediate surroundings, which she intuitively translates into

Pauline's second studio, Allanbank, set up for Open Studio Exhibition, 1998. Photo: Keith Tidball

Open Studio Exhibition, 1998,
textile work by Pauline Burbidge,
sculpture by Charles Poulsen.
Photo: Keith Tidball

Open Studio Exhibition, 1998,
textile work by Pauline Burbidge,
sculpture by Charles Poulsen.
Photo: Keith Tidball

fabric and stitch. Reflections are a constant theme, as is the gently meditative movement of water. Her palette has become simple and Japanese-like, limiting the colors to blue, black, and white. She says, "When I am engaged and totally absorbed in my work, I find myself in a space that has no words but simply works with visual language." *Whiteadder*, made in 1995 (see pages 27 and 51), saw the addition of clear plastic covering the surface. This held down the loose threads and small slithery pieces of fabric, but also gave an additional light-reflective surface to the work. It was secured by a final "scribble" of quilting stitches.

Throughout her career Pauline has always worked on a series of pieces which follow a similar theme. As her work progresses in this new pastoral environment, so it becomes increasingly lyrical. Still working with the square grid, the additional sashing acts to frame a passing moment in time. *Paxton Study I* (see page 48) and *Paxton Study II* (see page xvii), both made in 1997, depict playful waves whipped up against the riverbank. The darker pools of color suggest the threat of undercurrents lurking beneath the surface and a reminder that a gentle meandering river can swiftly turn into a raging torrent.

A tradition in quiltmaking is to commemorate an event which otherwise would be forgotten. A series called *Colour Study I*, 1997 (see page 64), and *Colourbank*, 1998 (see page 120), do just that. Instead of using fragments of clothes as an act of remembrance, petals from garden flowers are collected and painstakingly arranged under clear plastic (like pressed flowers in a book) to record the passing season. This new work coincided with the move to Scotland and long, country walks that familiarized Pauline with a different landscape. Feathers and leaves have also been carefully collected, graded by color and size, then arranged in harmonious patterns. These quilts using found objects are produced alongside her Reflections work but evolve at a gentler pace.

Pauline Burbidge is both an artist who creates lyrical quilts and a designer craftsperson who shows meticulous attention to detail. Alongside Nancy Crow and Michael James, she is part of a significant group of stitched textile artists that have emerged in the last quarter of the twentieth century. Their creativity comes through the discipline of quiltmaking and is traditionally inspired. Through their virtuosity there has been a renewed interest in the subject leading to specialized galleries, exhibitions, and publications. *Quilt Studio* provides an essential source of design and practical information and also gives insight into the career of an exceptional quiltmaker.

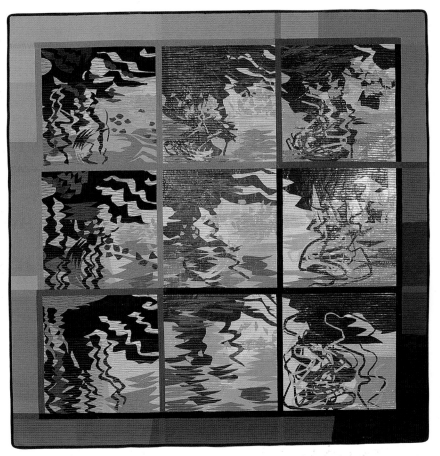

Paxton Study II, 1997, 53" × 53" (135 cm × 135 cm). Photo: Keith Tidball

Michele Walker studied graphic design and combines careers in textiles and publishing. She began making quilts in 1976 and has played a significant role in the artistic development of quiltmaking in Great Britain. She has written several books, notably The Complete Book of Quiltmaking *(Knopf) and* The Passionate Quilter *(Trafalgar Square). Michele Walker's own work combines traditional techniques with plastic materials that challenge the meaning and association of the word* quilt. *Her work is represented in major museum collections and exhibitions.*

Mirrored Steps (detail). See full quilt on page 85. Photo: John Coles, Cornwall

TECHNIQUES

The Workshops in the following chapters are divided into the four basic quiltmaking techniques I use—pieced patchwork, appliqué, quilting, and fabric dyeing and painting. In each, you will work alongside me through a series of samples that will help you master essential skills. A complete beginner, by working through and practicing each exercise, can quickly become proficient. If you are an experienced quiltmaker you should be able to handle all the projects with confidence, skipping over those that practice techniques with which you are most familiar and concentrating on those that are new to you. Do, however, read through each chapter, with an eye open for different ways of approaching familiar quiltmaking tasks.

The techniques presented here are meant to guide you, helping you speed up the technical processes involved in quiltmaking so that you can happily turn your attention to the design aspects of your work. But keep in mind that rules are made to be broken—if you find a better way to work that gives you faster, easier, or more satisfying results, use it. I feel that the nature of learning is to study every avenue open to you and work out the techniques that suit you best.

PART ONE

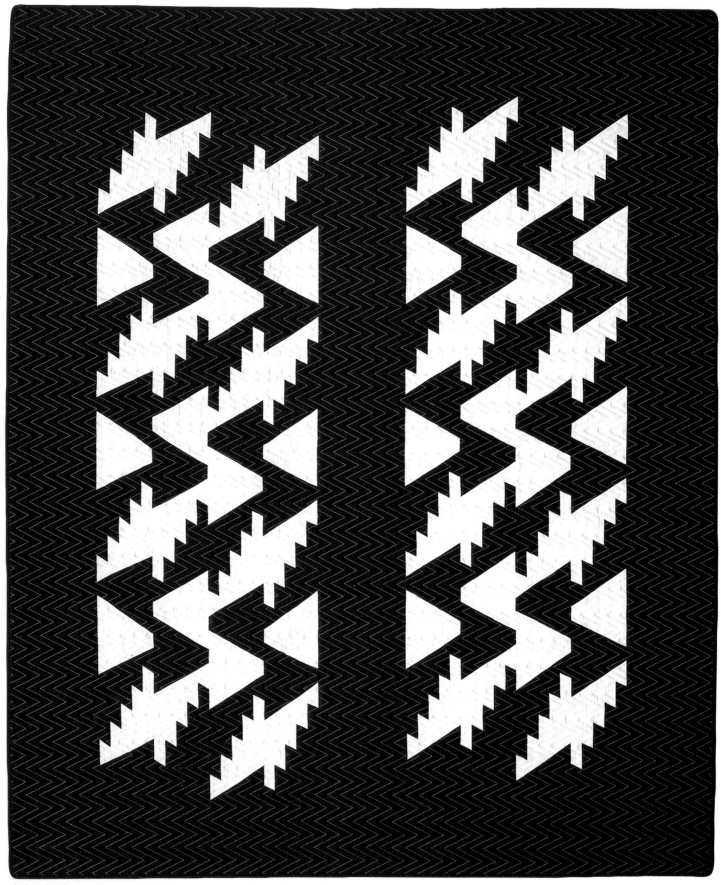

Black and White Bars II, 1986, 54" × 64" (137 cm × 160 cm). Photo: John Coles, Cornwall

Pieced Patchwork Workshop | CHAPTER 1

Pieced patchwork, or *piecing*, is simply the sewing together of two pieces of fabric either by hand or machine, using seams. Piecing can be as straightforward as sewing a series of identical squares together. Far more complex designs can be pieced, provided the same ordered, methodical procedure is followed. Piecing is particularly appropriate for quilt designs that use straight lines, sharp, crisp shapes, and hard-edged geometry. *Heron* on page 56 and *Pyramid II* on page 78 are both good examples.

   In this Workshop, we will work on several simple projects that cover the range of skills needed for successful piecing—making templates, cutting, and sewing basic shapes together. We will also practice the more complicated aspects of piecing—piecing acute angles, setting in corners, and sewing curves.

Black and White Bars II (detail). Photo: John Coles, Cornwall

WORKSHOP SUPPLIES

- General drawing equipment, including hard and soft pencils, chalk pencil, pencil sharpener, eraser, ruler
- General sewing equipment, including sewing machine

- Paper and fabric scissors
- Glue stick
- Graph paper, a few sheets with a square grid and a few with an isometric grid
- Thin cardboard for making templates

- Cutting mat and rotary cutter
- Iron and ironing board
- 1 yd (1 m) each black and white 100-percent-cotton fabric, preferably plain weave, prewashed

MAKING TEMPLATES

For Project 1, you will need a square template, as described here. Later projects will require other shapes and sizes but the method of making the templates is the same. To make a square template:

1. Draw a 2″ (5 cm) square onto graph paper and cut it out.
2. Glue the square down onto thin cardboard, leaving a little space around all edges.
3. Measure ¼″ (0.75 cm) beyond the graph-paper square. This adds a seam allowance. Draw a second, outer square around the graph paper directly onto the cardboard ¼″ (0.75 cm) from the inner square on all sides. Cut out the large square. This cardboard template is used to mark the fabric and cut out the nine-patch blocks, including seam allowance, ready for piecing.

Seam Allowance

Most quiltmakers use a ¼″ (0.75 cm) seam allowance. Before making your templates, however, check the distance between the needle and the outer edge of the foot on your sewing machine. This should be the width of your seam allowance. It is typically ¼″ (0.75 cm) but some machines vary.

For speed and accuracy, use a quilter's ruler with a ¼″ (0.75 cm) line along the length of it to mark the outer square. Match the ¼″ (0.75 cm) line to the edge of the graph paper and then draw the outside line, delineating the seam allowance.

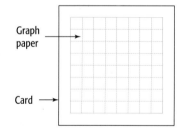

Graph paper →

Card →

Project 1 | **Nine-Patch Block**

This is one of the simplest quilting blocks to make and teaches the most basic of skills—sewing a straight seam.

1. Use the cardboard template described above to mark and cut out five fabric squares in black and four in white, keeping the grain of the fabric running in the same direction on each square (as shown beside Step 5). For this project, it is easiest to use scissors to cut out the squares, since we need so few of them. We will practice with rotary cutting equipment later in this chapter.
2. Lay out the squares in the order in which you wish to piece them.
3. Pick up the first pair of squares from the top row of the block, put right sides together, and stitch. Return to block. Pick up the stitched pair and the remaining top-row square, put right sides together, and stitch. Return to block. Repeat systematically with the middle and bottom rows. Press all seams open.
4. Place the top and middle rows right sides together, pinning to match the seams that cross over. Also pin the beginning and end of the seam line. Sew the rows together. In the same way, add the bottom row.
5. Press vertical seams open to complete the nine-patch block.

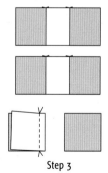

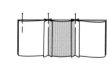

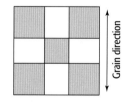

Grain direction

Step 3   Step 4   Step 5

Project 2 | **Rectangular Strip Block**

Like the nine-patch block, sewing a rectangular strip block allows you to practice simple piecing with right-angled seams.

1. Make a strip template by drawing a 10″ by ½″ (25 cm × 1.5 cm) rectangle onto graph paper. Paste this onto thin cardboard and add seam allowance around the outside.

2. Mark and cut five strips in black and five in white, matching the grain to the length of the template.

3. Lay out the strips as shown. Arrows denote the direction in which you will sew. If you sew all the seams in one direction, the block will curve to one side. Instead, sew alternating seams in opposite directions as shown.

4. Sew strips in pairs, right sides together, with the white strip on top of the dark. Press seams open. Return pairs to layout.

5. Pin the first two pairs together and sew, still with the white strips on top. This will ensure that alternate seams are sewn in opposite directions. Continue systematically, adding pairs of strips until block is complete. Press all seams open.

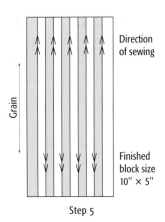

Direction of sewing

Grain

Finished block size 10" × 5"

Step 5

Measure the block to check that your piecing is accurate. It should measure 10" × 5" (25 cm × 15 cm), plus seam allowance around all four sides. Without practice, it's not unusual for measurements to be off—if you take the tiniest bit more or less on each seam, the effect quickly multiplies. If you get into the habit of checking that your seam allowances are accurate, your blocks will always measure up perfectly.

Project 3 | **Nine-Patch Diamond Block**

This project is excellent for practicing precision piecing. So far we have worked only with simple right-angled seams. The seams in this diamond block cross over at an angle, requiring extra skill to join the shapes.

1. Using isometric graph paper, draw a diamond shape measuring 2½" (6.5 cm) on each side. Cut this out, paste it to cardboard, and add the seam allowance. Cut out the whole template.

2. Mark and cut out five diamonds in black and four in white fabric, keeping the grain in line with the points.

3. Lay out the diamonds in the order in which you wish to piece them. Rows will be pieced in a similar way to the nine-patch block in Project 1.

4. Pick up two diamonds and place right sides together as shown, with the raw edges crossing the seam line. Sew together. Do not be tempted to match the points of the diamonds together. This is a common mistake. Since you are not working with right-angled seams, the seam should not line up. Add the next diamond to the stitched block to complete the first row. Repeat systematically to complete rows 2 and 3. Press seams open.

5. Put rows 1 and 2 right sides together. There are two points where the seams need to match: at the stitching line, i.e. ¼" (0.75 cm) in from the raw edges, and where they cross over. Place pins at these points and at either end of the seam before sewing. In the same way, add row 3.

6. Press seams open to complete the block.

If you do not have isometric graph paper, draw the diamond with 60° angles at the top and bottom points and 120° angles at the side points.

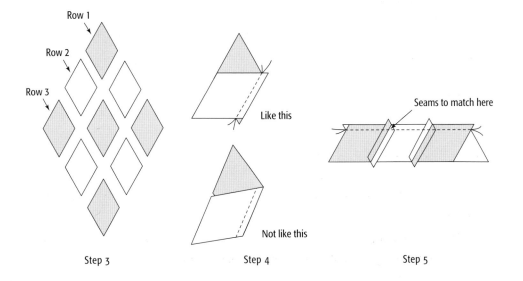

Row 1

Row 2

Row 3

Like this

Not like this

Seams to match here

Step 3

Step 4

Step 5

To avoid having the black fabric show through the white at the seams, either:
- Press the seams toward the black fabric. If you are using a heavyweight fabric, this may result in seams that are too bulky.
- Find the small black triangle that shows up the most and cut it out of the seam. This still leaves an even ¼" (0.75 cm) seam allowance intact. Do not cut the fabric shorter than the ¼" (0.75 cm) seam allowance.

To piece a shape like my design D, extra seams need to be added. Breaking up the design in this way (below) makes it possible to piece this unusual shape in fabric.

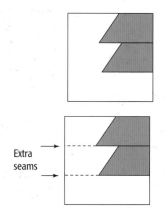

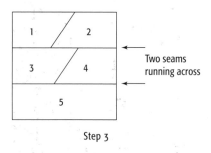

Extra seams

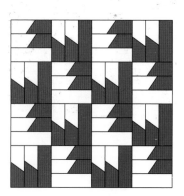

Step 3

Piecing Basics

To piece a quilt or patchwork project you will always need three key tools:

- Plan drawing: a graph-paper drawing of a single block, drawn to actual size.
- Templates: actual-size cutting guides, including seam allowances, made out of thin cardboard and graph paper.
- Layout diagram: drawing of multiple blocks showing repeating block pattern and serving also as a color reference. This can be small-scale, rather than actual size.

A sample layout

Project 4 | Design Your Own Block for Piecing

If you design your own block around these guidelines you will be pushed into a position of having to piece unusual shapes that you will not find in traditional quilt patterns. This will open up many other design possibilities to you.

1. Draw four 6" (15 cm) squares on graph paper.
2. In each square, take a ruler and pencil and draw a shape that has one or two sharp angles. Make sure the lines begin and end on the edges of the square.

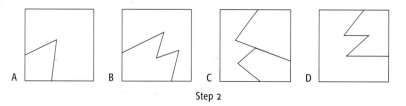

Step 2

3. Review your shapes to decide how you will piece them. It may be necessary to add extra seams or to simplify your designs. Work out an order of piecing and number the shapes in this order. Shown below is how I decided to piece design D.
4. Choose one of your designs and draw it twice on graph paper. Keep one drawing as a record, showing the order of piecing. From the other, cut the numbered shapes out and paste them down on thin cardboard, adding seam allowance, to make templates.

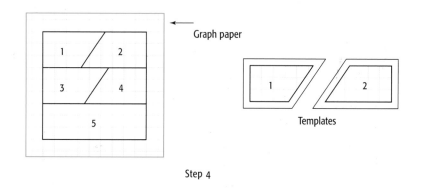

Graph paper

Templates

Step 4

5. Referring back to your original drawing, use the templates to cut out the piecing shapes from fabrics of your choice.
6. Stitch the block together, using appropriate piecing methods from Projects 1 to 3. If you pieced these projects together successfully, you should have no trouble making up similar designs of your own. Keep your layout diagrams and templates together in a bag or envelope for future use.
7. Work out a simple repeating-block layout using one of the designs you created. You can do this by photocopying or redrawing multiples of your graph-paper designs, or you can sew up several blocks in fabric. As an example, here I have repeated 16 blocks, turning every other block at right angles. For the turned blocks, the colors are reversed—I used darks where the light colors are in the original blocks. Experiment by moving your blocks around into different positions. Many different layouts can be created using the same block. (See Chapter 8 for further exploration of repeating patterns.)

The Final Pyramid, 1982, 42" × 42" (107 cm × 107 cm). Photo: John Coles, Cornwall

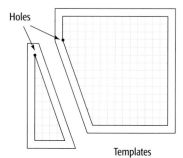

Holes

Templates

Step 1

OTHER ESSENTIAL PIECING TECHNIQUES

So far we have explored key piecing techniques, working with simple patchwork shapes. Once you gain confidence in easy cutting and piecing and in sewing straight seams, there are several other techniques you can practice to improve your skills and give you more sewing options.

Piecing Acute Angles

Sharp points created by acute angles can be troublesome to piece accurately. Here is a method that can help.

1. Make holes in your template on both sides of the seam exactly where the point needs to match.
2. Using a chalk pencil, mark through these holes onto the cut-out fabric shape.
3. To piece, place right sides together and match the two chalk dots. Pin carefully along the seam line to hold the fabric in place before sewing.

Piecing Sharp Points

Even for experienced quiltmakers, it is tricky to piece shapes with sharp points, like the one shown below. I use one of three methods, two of which involve adding additional seams.

1. Clip into the corner of the white fabric by almost ¼″ (0.75 cm). Sew up to this point and leave the machine needle down while lifting the machine foot. Rearrange the fabric and continue sewing in the new direction. Press the seams toward the black fabric.
2. Break the block up into three rather than the original two pieces by adding a straight seam into the corner (on the white fabric). Sew the two white pieces together from the edge of the block toward the center, leaving the last ¼″ (0.75 cm) of the seam unsewn. Sew in the same way as in Method 1. This time, clipping is not necessary, as the unsewn seam opens up instead of the clipped fabric.
3. Add additional seams as necessary to break up the design into simpler shapes. Note that this is only possible with larger-scale blocks. Sew as above.

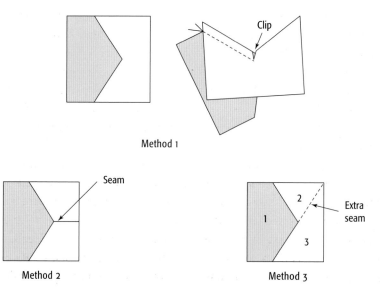

Clip

Method 1

Seam

Method 2

2

1

3

Extra seam

Method 3

Sewing Curved Seams

Curved seams can also be difficult to piece. The following tips can make them much easier. Generally, the gentler the curve, the easier it is to piece, so practice first with gradual curves like the one below.

1. Re-create the plan drawing and template shown, beginning with a 6″ (15 cm) square. Before cutting up the drawing to make the templates, make two balance marks at points that divide the curved line approximately into thirds. Pierce the templates where the curved seam will begin and end.
2. Cut the shapes out in fabric, transferring both the balance marks and the beginning and ending points onto the fabric with a chalk pencil. Clip the curved edge of the white fabric seam in a few places, making the clips less than ¼″ (0.75 cm) deep.
3. Place fabric pieces right sides together and pin, matching all chalk marks. Sew the seam carefully, with the white fabric on top. Press the seams toward the black fabric.

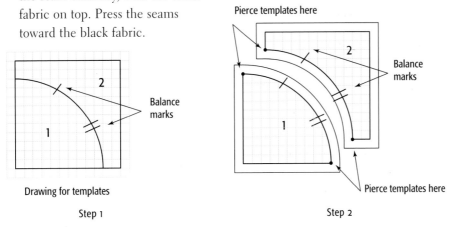

Drawing for templates

Step 1

Pierce templates here

Balance marks

Pierce templates here

Step 2

Fabric Grain

The true grain of fabric runs parallel to the selvages (the tightly woven edges of the cloth) and the warp yarns. The warp and weft are the yarns that make up the woven cloth. The warp yarns run parallel to the selvages, and the weft runs across the width of the fabric. As a quiltmaker, I find it sufficient to think of the grain line running parallel to either warp or weft yarns, thereby running parallel or at a right angle to it (the "true" grain runs parallel to the selvages). Quite often, when piecing blocks, you are working with tiny pieces of fabric and cannot see where the selvages are placed, but you can always see the weave texture.

Generally, when piecing quilt blocks, aim to keep the grain line running evenly throughout both the individual blocks and the overall quilt, either from left to right or from top to bottom. Do not allow it to go off course, as this will create difficulties in piecing. Moreover, it can cause the finished quilt top to stretch away from its intended rectangular or square shape.

However, there are two exceptions to this rule. First, when working with stripes (as in the rectangular strip block in Project 2 on pages 4 and 5), it is best to keep the grain running parallel to the stripes, regardless of the direction the stripes run in your design. If the stripes are off grain, they will stretch when you stitch them and you will end up with a distorted shape that will not fit into your other pieced areas. Second, if you are piecing diamonds together, it is much easier to keep the grain line always running into the points of the diamond, regardless of the overall direction of the quilt design.

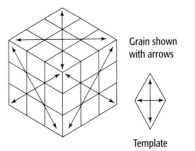

Grain shown with arrows

Template

Exception to the grain line rule

Rotary Cutting

So far in this Workshop, we have been working with single blocks that require little cutting. Once you begin creating full quilts, however, you will find that using a rotary cutter and cutting mat allows you to cut multiple shapes quickly, easily, and with wonderful accuracy. The sharp, circular blade cuts swiftly and neatly through all cotton fabrics. Take care when you first start practicing with a rotary cutter—the blade is extremely sharp!

Cutting Strips

Equal-width strips can be cut very easily and speedily using a rotary cutter and a quilt-maker's transparent ruler with measurement markings along its length. Simply match the required width to the raw edge and cut the first strip. Slide the ruler down the fabric, again matching to the required width, and cut the next strip. Repeat, making multiple strips with absolute accuracy and ease.

Cutting Through Multiple Layers

The rotary cutter will cut through three or four layers of fabric. Simply mark the required shapes onto the top layer of fabric and cut through several thicknesses. Try to mark the shapes in a logical order so that it is easy to cut them out using the ruler as a guide. Think in terms of cutting continuous lines rather than isolated shapes.

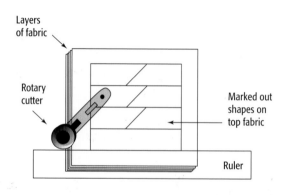

Layers of fabric

Rotary cutter

Marked out shapes on top fabric

Ruler

Cotton fabrics are ideal for cutting in layers because they cling together so well. It is possible to move and swivel multiple layers of fabric before making a new cut in another direction.

Once you have mastered the techniques described in this chapter, the design arena that opens up to you is broad and exciting. If you feel ready to start exploring design options, turn to Part Two and read Chapter 5 on strip piecing, Chapter 7 on geometric 3-D designs, or Chapter 8 on pattern and the repeating block. These chapters all provide ideas and inspirations to help you explore piecing techniques further.

Look closely, too, at the quilts that illustrate piecing. From geometric designs like Cubic Log Cabin (page 77) and Liquorice Allsorts (page 72) to pictorial quilts like Heron (page 56) and Egyptian Quilt (page 11), they will show you just how varied and versatile pieced designs can be.

Studio Quilts

Egyptian Quilt and *Egyptian Scarab* were among the first pieced quilts I made. I planned and designed them on graph paper, as shown below. This drawing was useful in many ways. I used it to work up the design, choose shapes, and decide colors. I also used it to work out how I would piece the fabrics together. When I moved from the small to the larger quilt, the drawing helped me scale up each shape correctly.

Egyptian Quilt, 1979, 41″ × 46″ (104 cm × 117 cm). Photo: Pauline Burbidge

Egyptian Scarab (detail), 1978, 81″ × 95″ (206 cm × 241 cm). Photo: Pauline Burbidge

Graph paper design for *Egyptian Scarab*, 1977, 22″ × 18″ (56 cm × 45 cm). Photo: Pauline Burbidge

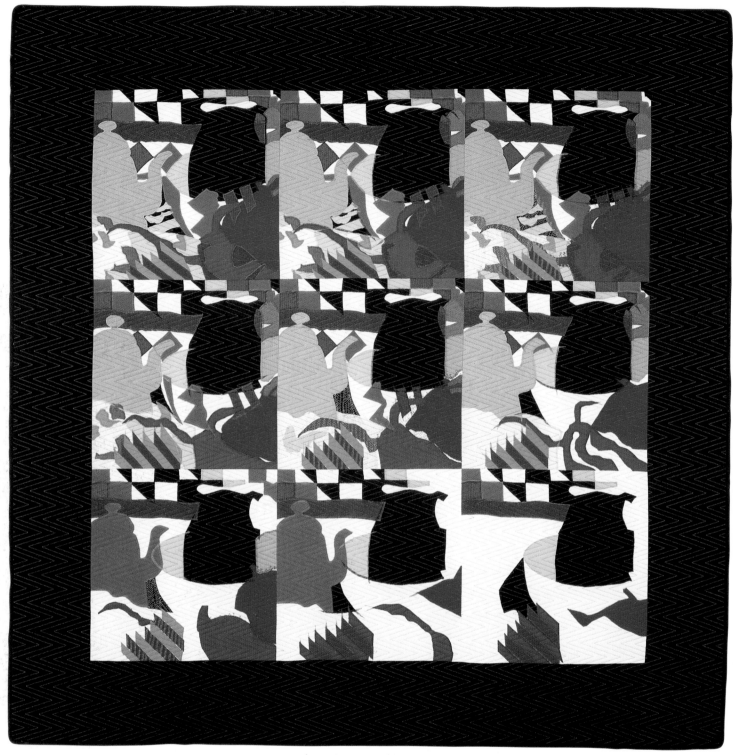

The Pink Teapot, 1987, 55" × 55" (140 cm × 140 cm). Photo: Keith Tidball

Appliqué Workshop | CHAPTER 2

Appliqué simply means applying one layer of fabric to another. Any shape can be cut out and applied to a backing fabric. Unlike piecing, appliqué is very free in form. The technique lends itself readily to designs using curved shapes.

In this Workshop, we will make several simple blocks to illustrate this very versatile quiltmaking style. We will practice both traditional hand appliqué and machine appliqué and collage. Try each of the projects that follow to discover which method you favor.

The Pink Teapot (detail). Photo: Keith Tidball

WORKSHOP SUPPLIES

- General drawing equipment, including hard and soft pencils, pencil sharpener, eraser, ruler
- General sewing equipment, including sewing machine and machine and hand threads

- Paper and fabric scissors
- Graph paper, plain white paper, tracing paper
- Sheet of tissue paper or Stitch 'n Tear
- Iron and ironing board

- ¼ yd (0.25 m) fusible web, such as Bondaweb or Wonder-Under
- ¼ yd (0.25 m) each black and white 100-percent-cotton fabric, preferably plain weave, prewashed

Project 5 | **Hand Appliqué Block**

Here we will make an 8″ (20 cm) appliqué block, sewing around curves. We will practice three simple appliqué stitches.

1. Draw an 8½″ (21.5 cm) square onto graph paper, cut it out, and use it as a paper pattern to cut out a white fabric base block. This includes a ¼″ (0.75 cm) seam allowance around outside edges.
2. Take a sheet of plain white paper and draw an 8″ (20 cm) square on it. Draw some simple curved shapes within the square.
3. Cut out the curved shapes and use them as templates. Pin them to the black fabric and cut around them, leaving at least a ¼″ (0.75 cm) seam allowance on all edges.
4. Fold the fabric over the edges of the first paper shape and tack in place. Press thoroughly, then remove the tacking stitches and the paper template. Keep the paper template for future use.

If there are shapes that flow into the edge of the block, leave them unturned. Once you are ready to sew your blocks together into a quilt, their edges will be turned under and sewn in with the seam allowance that surrounds the whole block.

Step 2

Step 3

Step 4

5. Pin the fabric shape to the base block and stitch into place using one of the following three stitches: slip (or hem) stitch, blanket stitch, or oversewing stitch. You could try out all three on this sample block to decide which method you prefer. The drawings illustrate how the stitches are made.
6. Position and stitch the remaining fabric shapes in place to complete the block.

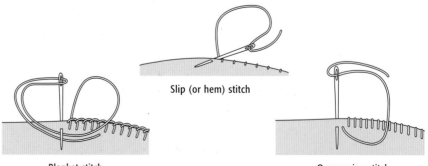

Slip (or hem) stitch

Blanket stitch

Oversewing stitch

Project 6 | **Machine Appliqué Block or Fabric Collage**

Here we will practice machine stitching onto shapes that have been anchored with fusible web, such as Bondaweb or Wonder-Under. With this method, any shape can be cut out and used without turning under seam allowances.

1. Use the same 8½" (21.5 cm) graph paper pattern from Project 5 to cut out a base block in white fabric. Again, draw your design onto an 8" (20 cm) square of white paper, using similar curved shapes.
2. Take a sheet of tracing paper and copy the whole block, including the outer edges of the square, onto it.
3. Flip the tracing over, reverse side up, and place the fusible web, smooth side up, over it. Trace the shapes, adding seam allowances on the outer edges as necessary. Try to group the shapes fairly close together on the fusible web.

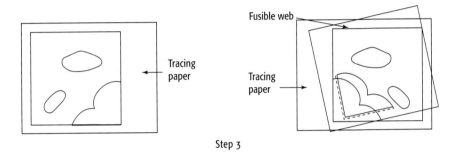

Step 3

4. Cut the fusible web roughly around the group of shapes and iron it as one unit onto the black fabric.
5. Cut out the separate shapes and peel off the backing paper. Place them in position on the white fabric base block, using the tracing paper as a guide. Press with a hot iron to secure.

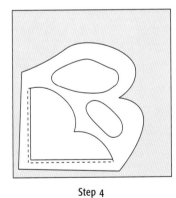

Step 4   Step 5

6. To prepare the block for machine stitching, you will need to strengthen the single layer of backing fabric to prevent the stitches from wrinkling the fabric. Use one of two methods.
   • Tack a piece of tissue paper or Stitch 'n Tear behind the whole block before stitching. This can be torn off after stitching.
   • Iron a second layer of fusible web onto the reverse side of the block, covering areas that are of a single thickness. This material will be permanent, but it will give the block substance to hold all types of stitching.
7. Sew the curved pieces to the base block using any of the machine stitching methods described in the section that follows. You may want to make several blocks to try out different stitches. Satin stitch and zigzag are good choices for beginners.

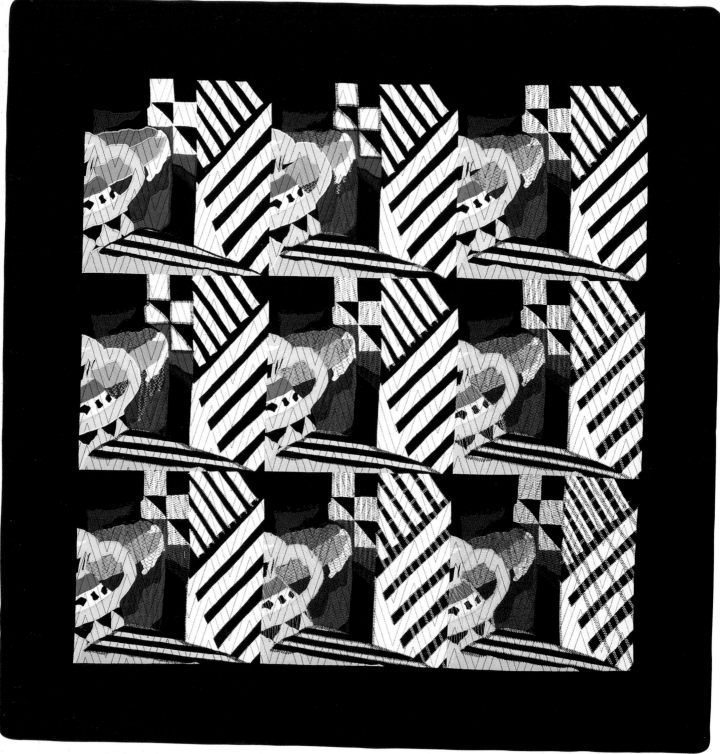

Kate's Vase, 1987, 35" × 35" (89 cm × 89 cm). Photo: John Coles, Cornwall

OTHER ESSENTIAL APPLIQUÉ TECHNIQUES

Machine Stitches

There are four basic machine stitches for appliqué.

Satin Stitch

Set your machine to a close zigzag stitch. Before working on your block, try out on scrap fabric to adjust your stitch to the required width and density. Use an open-fronted embroidery stitch so that you can see the edge of the fabric clearly. This stitch is ideal for sewing around appliquéd shapes. It forms a solid line, so choose your thread color with care. (See the detail from *Kate's Vase* to the right.)

Zigzag Stitch

This is a more open stitch than satin stitch—you can see the fabric through the stitching. Like satin stitch, zigzag can be used to sew around the edges of appliquéd shapes, resulting in a less solid line. You can also use zigzag to sew over the entire surface, trapping the appliqué pieces beneath the stitches (see Straight Machine Stitching on page 18.) With this method, it is easy to change the color and tone of a block by choosing a contrasting thread color.

Kate's Vase (detail). Photo: John Coles, Cornwall

Free Machining

If you want a free and easy stitching style, free machining is for you. It is like drawing with a needle and thread. You can send the stitches in any direction and break free of the orderly rows that other stitches create. To start, simply attach a darning foot and lower the feed dog. Here are three free machining styles to try:

- You can create a feathery line around shapes.
- Or a line that resembles rough scribbles.
- Or stitch freely over the entire shape.

If you have not tried free machining before, practice by removing the thread from your machine (both top and bobbin). Keep the needle speed regular and stitch fairly quickly, moving the fabric gently as you go.

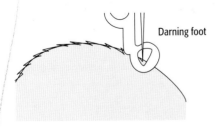

Darning foot

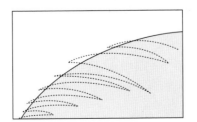

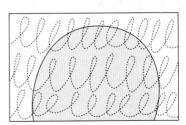

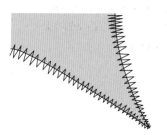

Straight Machine Stitching

Sew simple rows of straight stitching, repeated close together, over the entire shape and the area that surrounds it. By switching threads often, interesting color variations can easily be achieved with this method of stitching.

Sewing Points and Curves

So far, we have practiced sewing only very simple shapes. Once you get started on your own blocks, you will want to stitch more unusual shapes, such as points or curves. The techniques are easy, both by hand and machine, but it takes a little practice to achieve good results.

Sewing Curves by Machine

Sew in short stages, stopping every few stitches. Leaving the needle down on the outer edge of the fabric, lift the presser foot to adjust the fabric. Continue around the curve, repeating this stop-and-start action.

Sewing Points by Machine

Gradually decrease the width of the stitching toward the point, so that you are using very small stitches—down to o—as you approach it. Leaving the needle down, swivel the fabric at the point and then begin to stitch in the new direction. Increase the width gradually again as you stitch away from the point.

Sewing Points by Hand

Use a paper template to fold the fabric over, as described earlier (see page 14). Tack the fabric over the edges. Before reaching the point, fold the fabric over as shown and then arrange the side folds. This will make a good sharp point. Press well, remove the paper template and tacking stitches, and stitch the shape onto the backing or base fabric. For inverted points, clip the fabric almost as far as the paper template. Then fold and tack.

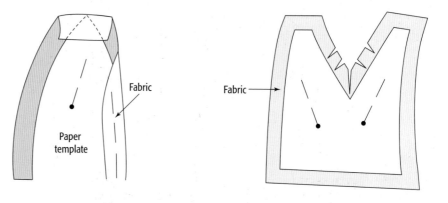

In the projects in this Workshop we practiced appliquéing very simple shapes with easy, gradual turns. Yet both machine and hand appliqué can involve much more complex shapes. With both hand and machine appliqué, you can achieve a range of effects. The techniques behind them are easy to learn but take practice to perfect.

Studio Quilt

I find appliqué a very free method of working that allows me to explore all kinds of shapes, including curved pieces, and fine lines, as in reverse appliqué. The quilt shown here—as well as several others in this book—illustrates the diversity of the technique. *Nottingham Reflections* on page 108 and *Intercut Fish–Harmony* on page 86 are two more examples. *Kate's Vase* on page 16 was the first appliqué quilt I made, after making several pieced quilts. Look closely at the detail photograph to see several machine appliqué stitches described in this Workshop.

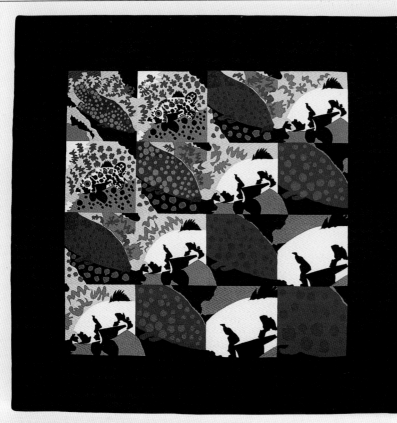

Joining Forces, 1989, 86" × 86" (218 cm × 218 cm). Photo: Keith Tidball

Joining Forces (detail). Photo: Keith Tidball

Reflections III, 1995, 47" × 47" (119 cm × 119 cm). Photo: Keith Tidball

Quilting Workshop | CHAPTER 3

What is quilting? In this chapter we take it back to basics and define it as any form of stitching that attaches three layers of material together. In the Workshop we will work through several quilting techniques, making small-scale samples with each. At the same time, I will explain how to use the methods with full-size quilts.

This is an experimental Workshop, covering traditional techniques but also inventing new ones. From hand running stitches through large-scale stab stitching to embellishing with buttons, beads, and sequins, you will find that there is much more to quilting than just holding the layers of a quilt together.

Reflections III (detail). Photo: Keith Tidball

WORKSHOP SUPPLIES

- General sewing equipment, including sewing machine, thimbles, needles of various sizes

- Quilting foot and guide, darning foot, open-fronted embroidery foot

- 14″ (36 cm) wide quilting hoop or quilting frame (see pages 22 and 29)

- Tracing paper, thin cardboard

- 1 yd (1 m) muslin (U.S.) or cotton calico (U.K.), prewashed

- 1 yd (1 m) plain woven white cotton fabric, prewashed

- 1 yd (1 m) fine woven white cotton fabric, such as cotton lawn, prewashed

- 9″ (23 cm) square of each of two colored cotton fabrics, prewashed

- ¼ yd (0.25 m) of each of four or five types of batting (or wadding) for experimentation

- White machine thread and thicker cotton thread for hand sewing

- Selection of sequins, buttons, and beads for embellishments

Project 7 | **Hand-Quilted Blocks**

Here we divide a square of fabric into four quarters and try out three different ways of quilting—running stitch, stab stitch, and embellishing. In the last quarter we will make further experiments. Compare each, both in terms of the ease with which you mastered the stitch and the final look on the fabric.

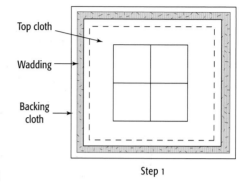

1. In the center of a 20" (50 cm) square of plain cotton fabric draw four 6" (15 cm) squares in pencil. Cut the muslin (or calico) for the backing fabric. Cut a medium-weight batting into slightly larger squares, approximately 21" (53 cm). Tack the three layers together.

   Top cloth

   Wadding

   Backing cloth

   Step 1

2. Stretch the "quilt sandwich" over the quilting hoop so that you can work with ease on one complete square. A C-clamp (G-clamp) is sometimes useful to hold the hoop still while you quilt.

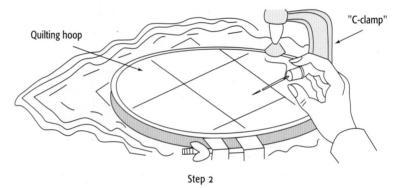

Quilting hoop

"C-clamp"

Step 2

Running Stitch

3. In the first square, try a traditional quilting stitch—a small running stitch. Use two thimbles, one on the middle finger of each hand. To start, use one of two methods. Look at the drawings when you follow these instructions:

   - Using quilting thread, tie a small knot and, from the right, or top, side of the quilt, feed the needle and thread between the batting and the top cloth for about 1" (2.5 cm). Bring the needle back up to the surface at the beginning of the quilting line. Tug the knot down through the top layer of fabric so that it disappears into the batting.
   - Make a backstitch (as in the second illustration), then send the needle down through the center of that stitch, thereby splitting the thread. Bring the needle back up just a short distance from the backstitch.

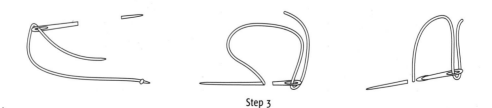

Step 3

4. You are now ready to stitch. Make one stitch at a time, holding one hand underneath and one on top. Use the top thimble to push the needle, and use the corner edge of the bottom thimble to push the point of the needle back up. The aim is to obtain an evenly spaced small running stitch on both sides of the fabric. With practice, you can stitch fairly rapidly.

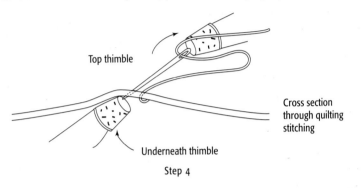

Top thimble

Cross section through quilting stitching

Underneath thimble

Step 4

5. On the last stitch, take the needle down to the underneath side. Then return it up through the center of the stitch, splitting the thread. Take the needle through from the end of the stitch and feed it between the batting and the top fabric for about 1" (2.5 cm). Cut the thread. Once you have developed a rhythm of stitching, try one of the marked patterns later in this chapter (see page 24).

As you gain confidence with single stitches, try "stacking" your stitches—collecting several stitches onto the needle before pulling the thread through. For some quilters, this method speeds up the process and creates nice, evenly spaced stitches.

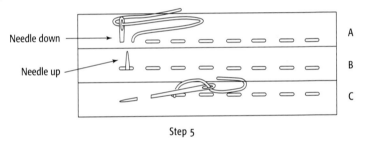

Needle down — A

Needle up — B

C

Step 5

Stab Stitch

6. Much larger stitches called stab stitches can be used for quilting, using a thick cotton thread. This method makes the quilting go a little faster. Adjust the quilt sandwich in the hoop so that the second complete square is easy to work with. Thread a large-eyed needle with a thick cotton thread. Do not knot the thread.

7. Begin stitching, as in the previous sample, by passing the needle under the surface of the top fabric and splitting the yarn of the first stitch to secure it.

8. Beginning from underneath the hoop, make the two simple up and down actions shown.

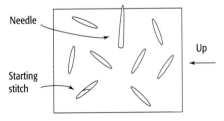
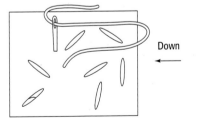

Needle

Up

Down

Starting stitch

Step 8

Making Simple Quilting Designs

Some of the simplest and most effective quilting designs are easily marked onto fabric using just a pencil and ruler or a curved template. Each of the designs shown here can be rotated, mirrored, or staggered as you move from block to block in a full quilt. For example, horizontal lines can become vertical in alternating blocks.

Quilting stencils are very easy to use. This traditional design is easy to achieve using a commonly available plastic stencil or creating your own stencil with thin cardboard. With chalk or a pencil, simply draw around the outside edge and then mark the inner dots through the holes in the stencil. Remove the stencil and complete the quilting lines by joining the dots.

Use the same tracing paper plan drawing you created for the original block design to mark your quilting design. Copy the design onto thin cardboard and use as a stencil. Since it's easier to draw around shapes than to create quilting lines by joining dots, here is a technique you can try with symmetrical designs. Take a quarter of the symmetrical design and make a template out of it on thin cardboard. In the design shown here, you will then need to dot and fill in only two lines.

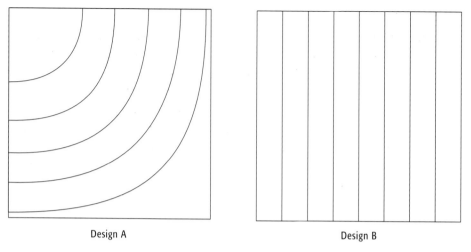

Design A   Design B

Two sample quilting designs

Design B, put into repeat

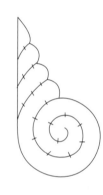

A simple quilting marking template

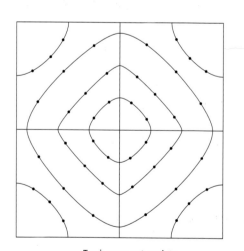

Tracing paper template

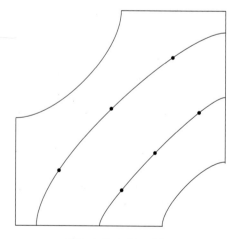

Thin cardboard template

Embellishments

9. Use this stitch to hand stitch embellishments, such as buttons, beads, short strings of beads, or small squares of felt or fabric, at random intervals onto the third square of your quilt sample blocks. Choose a thickness of thread appropriate to the embellishments you are using. If in doubt, try a hand quilting thread or a thick cotton thread. The stitch will be the same as stab stitch and the length of stitch will be appropriate to the button or bead you are using. You could also stitch down strips of narrow ribbon, either flat or rounded. Experiment, too, with stitching tiny swatches of colored fabrics to the top surface, or stitching transparent fabric over the entire square. Experiments like these are not only fun, but allow you to see the effects of simple techniques that you can later apply to full-size projects.

Other Experiments

10. Use the fourth square of your quilt sandwich to try new alternative ways of joining the three layers together. I suggest French knots or large cross stitches. Try tying thick yarn or narrow ribbon through all three layers. This is a simple, traditional method of quilting, a popular alternative to the running stitch. You will still find woolen quilts or thick tweeds tied in this manner.

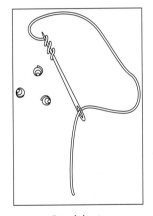

French knots

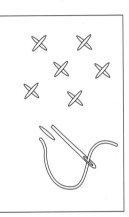

Cross stitch

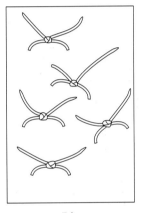

Tying

As you stitch you will have one hand under the frame and one on top. A 14" (36 cm) quilting hoop is excellent, as it allows you to reach all areas within it with ease.

Project 8 | **Machine-Quilted Blocks**

The quality of your quilting can vary tremendously depending upon the type of batting and the machine foot attachments used. The next series of samples is designed so that you can compare the different effects. Keep your samples to help in selecting materials for future projects.

1. To make a sample block, cut a 7" (18 cm) square of white cotton fabric. Cut an 8" (20 cm) square of selected batting and an 8" (20 cm) square of muslin or calico for the backing.
2. Mark two opposite edges of the 7" (18 cm) block with pencil dots at ½" (1.5 cm) intervals. Draw very faint lines to join these dots across the fabric. Pin this top fabric over the batting and the calico square, pinning all three layers together.
3. Stitch the block with a regular machine stitch and normal sewing machine foot. Sew each line in the same direction and remove the pins as you go.
4. Repeat Steps 1 to 3 using
   - Various types and weights of batting.
   - Different thicknesses of fabric, such as a heavy batting combined with a fine cotton on the top.
   - Various threads, such as thicker thread, metallic thread, cording.
   - A walking foot.

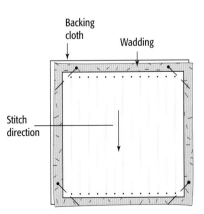

Backing cloth

Wadding

Stitch direction

Step 2

- A foot with a quilting guide. Instead of marking the entire fabric, just mark the first line and then match your guide to this.
- Various stitches, such as a narrow satin stitch, a zigzag stitch, a fancy wave stitch.

You could also try loosening the presser foot (if this is possible on your sewing machine) to see if the effect is different.

5. On the reverse of each sample, note the materials and tools you used for future reference.

Project 9 | **Sink Stitching by Machine**

Here, the aim is to hide the quilting stitches within the seam lines of the block. This technique, called *sink stitching*, takes practice, so use up as many sample blocks as you need before moving on to work on a finished quilt top.

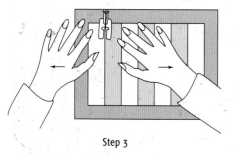

Step 3

1. Choose two colors of fabric. From the first fabric, cut four 1½" × 7" (4 cm × 18 cm) strips; from the second, cut three 1½" × 7" (4 cm × 18 cm) strips. Piece them together to form a 7" (18 cm) square block. Cut an 8" (20 cm) square of batting and fabric backing, and pin the three layers together.
2. Set up the machine with a regular stitch length, an open-footed embroidery foot, and, if possible, a slow speed setting.
3. Begin stitching within one of the seam lines. Use your hands as a frame around the sewing foot, easing the fabric slightly out to the sides. Take care not to push or pull the fabric from the back or front. The aim is to stitch exactly on top of the seam line, allowing the stitches to sink out of sight. Move on to the next seam. Sew each line in the same direction.

Project 10 | **Free-Motion Quilting**

Outline Quilting

This is another form of free-motion quilting, where the fabric itself acts as a guide. Make a quilt sandwich using a fabric with a bold pattern or motif for the top layer. Using the free-motion technique, follow the outline of the printed shapes. You can do exactly the same thing when quilting by hand, using a regular running stitch. To center your motif in the hoop, you may need to tack the edges of the block to scrap fabric, which allows you to secure your block in the hoop.

Free-motion, or *free-machine* quilting, is a wonderfully easy and liberating way to quilt. With free-motion stitching you can stitch in any direction. Think of it as a form of drawing, but here you are moving the paper (the fabric) rather than the pencil (the needle).

1. Set up your machine by dropping the feed dog and using a darning or embroidery foot. Set the stitch length to 0. Before threading the machine and bobbin, practice with no thread in place.
2. Hold the fabric firmly within 1" to 2" (2 cm to 4 cm) of the darning foot, moving it smoothly and freely below the needle in any direction you please. Keep the machine going at a fairly rapid, even speed.
3. Thinking of each of the examples shown as a continuous line of stitching, try these two free-motion designs.

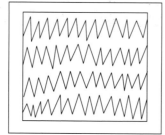 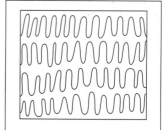

Step 3

Whiteadder, 1995, 33" × 33" (83 cm × 83 cm). Photo: Keith Tidball

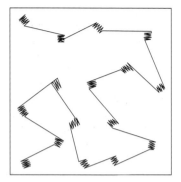

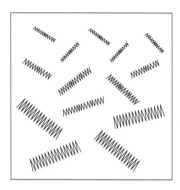

Quilting with satin stitch or
zigzag stitch

Project 11 | **Quilting with Satin Stitch or Zigzag Stitch**

Machine satin stitch or zigzag quilting can be used very effectively for quilting. Not only does this technique hold the layers of the quilt together firmly, but you can experiment with different placements from block to block or with different colored threads for a variety of visual effects. Here are some examples:

- Scatter 1″ (2.5 cm) rows of stitching at random over the block.
- Grade the stitches in both width and length of rows to give an illusion of depth.
- Create small dots from just a few satin stitches. Then move the fabric to the next site, leaving a trail of thread running between the dots. This technique works particularly well with normal cotton sewing thread.

OTHER ESSENTIAL QUILTING TECHNIQUES

The techniques we practiced in the previous projects were all used with single, small-scale sample blocks, designed to practice the various quilting techniques. Things begin to change when you are working on a large-scale quilt. It is no longer the single block that you are stitching, but a quilt that can measure 2 square yards (2 square m) or more. In this section we will explore ways to handle this amount of fabric, making it easier to maneuver around it.

Planning Large-Scale Quilting Projects

Once you have completed your quilt top blocks for a full-size quilt, take some time to plan how you are going to quilt. Think both in terms of the technique you will use and the overall design of the stitches. It is very helpful to pin your blocks to a wall as you complete them. Not only will this help you decide on the best arrangement for your blocks, but it will make it easier for you to start thinking about the quilting design.

Hand or Machine?

The first decision to make is whether to quilt by hand or by machine. What is your quilt for? Will you use it on a bed or as a wall hanging? I imagine that if you want to use it on a bed, you would like to give it a soft, comforting quality. Hand quilting or an open network of machine quilting are both fine for this. Large stab stitching or embellishments would obviously not be appropriate. Before you begin, think of the type of quilting you prefer—hand or machine. You are much more likely to finish the quilt using the technique you enjoy the most. Think, too, of the quilting design you have chosen and of the type of stitching that would best suit it.

Quilting Design

Before you decide on a specific quilting design, take time to view the quilt top in its entirety. You may want to leave your work pinned to a wall for several days, even weeks, repositioning blocks until you are pleased with the overall arrangement. Decide on the design, direction, and overall pattern of your quilting stitches. The key is to leave aside thoughts of the separate blocks and see the quilt as an integrated whole. A technique I use to help me decide on quilting lines is to draw proposed quilting lines onto sheets of tracing paper and pin them directly over the blocks. When you are ready, make a rough sketch of the overall design you have in mind. You will need to refer back to this once your quilt is in a frame or when you are working on smaller sections of the design.

Preparing to Quilt

If you have decided to quilt by hand, you can go ahead and join all the blocks together, completing your quilt top. If you are planning to quilt by machine, you will first need to divide the quilt top into manageable sections (see page 31, Step 1).

You now need to mark the quilting lines onto the quilt top. A chalk pencil is ideal for dark or medium-tone fabrics; a normal graphite pencil works well with lighter colors. Spread the quilt top out flat and proceed to mark the quilting lines. Refer back to page 24 to see other options for marking quilting lines.

Next, cut the batting and backing fabric. Cut about 1" (2.5 cm) larger on all sides than the quilt top. Lay the backing fabric and batting out flat on the floor or a table. Place the quilt top over this. Pat the quilt top flat. Avoid smoothing it out too much, as this will make the backing fabric pucker up. Pin and then baste all three layers firmly together.

Large-Scale Quilting by Hand

There are two options for hand quilting a full-size quilt. You can stretch your work on a frame or use a quilting hoop. If you are not ready to make the investment to buy your own frame, ask at your local quilt or fabric shop—many will allow you to come in and use their frames, particularly if you buy your fabric there or enroll for classes. To use the frame:

1. Tack or baste the two opposite edges of the quilt to the webbing on the frame. Roll some of the quilt around one pole.

Quilting Density

Whether working by hand or machine, it is important to keep the density of your quilting stitches even throughout the design, otherwise the quilt will not lie flat. This is particularly important with machine quilting. Quilting stitches can be a bit like gathering—they shrink the fabric up. If you have areas of dense stitching and others lightly quilted or unquilted, the work will buckle. Though not appropriate for most quilts, you might want to experiment with uneven densities—exploit the idea to make a three-dimensional quilt!

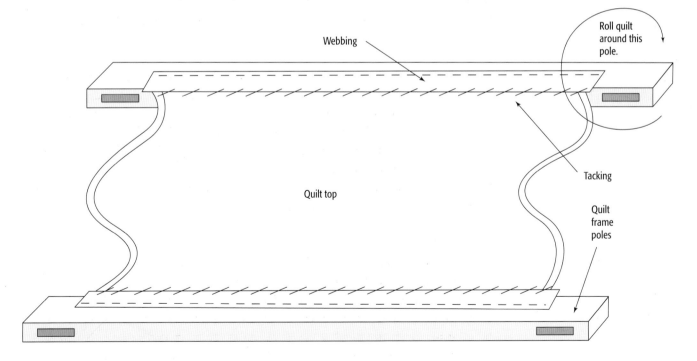

Step 1

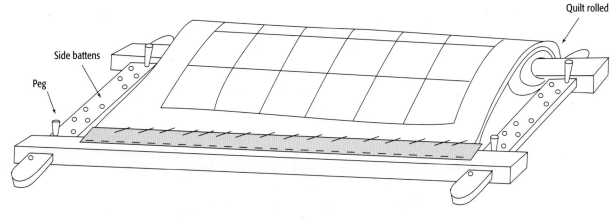

Side battens

Peg

Quilt rolled

Step 2

Many types of quilting frames are available, some of which are very sophisticated. This is an illustration of my own frame, which is very basic and very easy to make yourself from simple lengths of wood. This may be the best choice if you are just beginning to quilt and are unwilling to make a huge investment. My homemade frame has served me well for years.

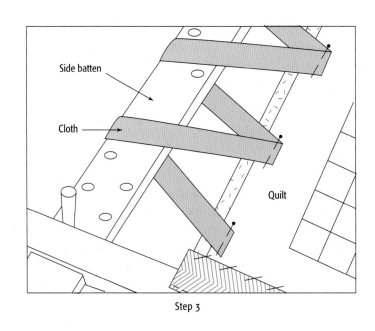

Side batten

Cloth

Quilt

Step 3

2. Place the side battens into position and peg so that the quilt is taut.

3. Pin some strips of scrap fabric to the edges of the quilt, looping them over and under the side battens as shown to make the edges of the quilt taut also. If necessary, hold the frame firmly in position with two C-clamps (G-clamps), which you can attach to a table of the right height.

Large-Scale Quilting by Machine

When making a large-scale quilt by machine, the hardest thing to manage is maneuvering the work within the space available on the sewing machine. It is very difficult to fold bulky fabric up tight enough to pass it through the narrow space between the motor and the needle. The difference between quilting the small-scale samples in the earlier machine-quilting projects and quilting a full-scale work is that you need to continuously reposition the bulk of the fabric as you work. This is the only way you will be able to put the stitches exactly where you want them to be. The bulky fabric wants to drag your work one way and then the other, altering the direction of the stitching or the evenness of the quilting stitches. It is a constant battle to stay even and keep on course. There are, however, several options to make it easier.

Machine Quilting in Sections

In my experience, it is impossible to stitch an entire quilt under the machine at once. This means that you need to divide up a large-scale quilt into two or three sections before you begin to quilt.

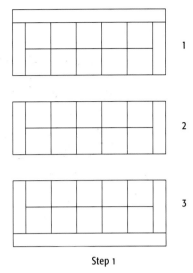

Step 1

1. Go back to your design wall, where you have pinned your blocks in place. Decide how best to divide the quilt top into sections for quilting. Sew the blocks together within each section, including the border. (See Step 1 at right.)

2. Refer back at this point to the quilting samples you created in Projects 8, 9, and 10 to help you decide what type of batting you will use and what type of stitching is appropriate. Thinner battings are ideal for machine quilting and make the quilt easier to stitch and handle. For beginners, a quilting design using straight lines with a straight machine stitch is the best choice. Pin or tack each section to the appropriately sized backing and batting materials. Proceed to stitch where you have marked, using your preplanned quilting design. Continue to quilt in large sections. If you would like a continuous border section, quilt the border area as a separate piece and join as shown below in Step 7.

3. Trim the batting and backing down to the outer edge of the seam allowance.

4. To join the quilted sections, carefully pin the seams together through all thicknesses, right sides of the quilt facing. Take care to match the points where necessary, and sew as a normal pieced seam, from the back of the quilt.

5. Press the seams open. This can be done without losing any of the batting thickness if you use cotton wadding. Thin out some of the batting trapped in the seam allowance to make it less bulky. Press again.

6. To cover the seam, cut a strip of fabric about 2″ (5 cm) wide out of the same fabric as your backing material. Make it a little longer than the length of the seam you are joining. Press over ⅜″ (1 cm) on either side of the strip, so that the strip now measures 1¼″ (3 cm)

7. Position the strip over the seam and hand-sew in place. Repeat to join additional sections.

If you are very determined—and an experienced seamstress—you may decide to quilt a large bed quilt all in one, thus avoiding having seams in your quilt. To make this possible, use a thin, lightweight batting. My recommendation, however, is to work in quilted sections—the seams can be hidden quite easily.

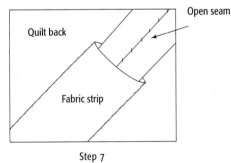

Step 7

Open seam

Quilt back

Fabric strip

Machine Quilting Block by Block

Quilting each block individually before joining them is another way to avoid problems caused by bulky fabrics when machine quilting. I used this method in several of my fabric collage pieces, such as *Tweed Reflections II* shown on page 32 and *Dancing Lines* on page 117. The sequence of photographs of the making of *Dancing Lines* on page 69 illustrates this technique.

1. Add batting and backing to each block. Machine quilt blocks individually, then trim them down to a uniform size.

Tweed Reflections II (detail). See full quilt on page iii. Photo: Keith Tidball

If you do not like the idea of a 1″ (2.5 cm) bar separating your blocks, you could make the top strip of fabric with broken-up fabric collage shapes, covering the butted seam. This technique is simple and allows more versatility of design. (See *Whiteadder* on page 27.)

2. Select the first two blocks from your design. Press a 1″ (2.5 cm) fabric strip (prepressed with fusible web) onto the back, joining the blocks together.
3. Turn the work to the front and press a second 1″ (2.5 cm) strip over the joint on the front.
4. Stitch over the top of the butted seam.
5. Repeat Steps 2 to 4 until all blocks are assembled.

Quilting block by block in this manner is much easier than machine quilting in a single piece or in sections. Inevitably, however, as you near completion, you will experience difficulty in handling the full quilt.

Before you begin, plan the easiest way to assemble your blocks. You may also want to incorporate hand quilting with machine quilting on large-scale quilts to make those last blocks easier to add.

Finishing the Quilt

One of the methods I have used most is to bind quilt edges with *bias* strips cut from fabric.

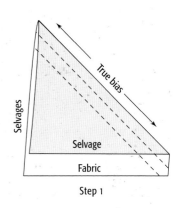

Step 1

1. Fold the fabric on the bias or cross grain.
2. Cut several strips of fabric 2¼″ (5.5 cm) wide, along the bias or cross grain.
3. Sew bias strips together end to end, forming a strip long enough to go around the whole edge of the quilt.
4. Press the joining seams open, then press the bias strip in half lengthwise right side out to give two raw edges on one side and a folded edge on the other side of the strip.
5. Place the binding on the front of the quilt, matching raw edges of binding to raw edges of the quilt. Begin sewing a short distance from the end of the bias strip to allow you to make the final join.
6. Before stitching the binding around the corner, clip the binding ¼″ (0.75 cm) in from the raw edges at a point ¼″ (0.75 cm) before the quilt corner, as shown. This clip will open up on the corner and allow you to ease the binding around the corner.
7. Turn the folded edge of the bias over to the back, and hand sew binding in place.

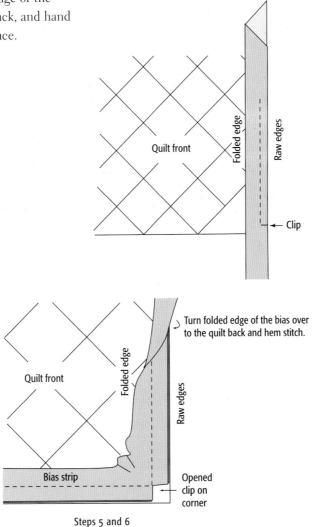

Steps 5 and 6

Hanging Quilts

To hang the quilt on a wall, I always sew two fabric sleeves, one on the top and one on the lower edge of the quilt back. I make the sleeves so that they finish at about 3″ (7.5 cm) wide. I sew them about 1½″ (4 cm) in from each side. This is deliberately shorter than the quilt width to allow the corner of the quilt to be folded back when the wood slat that holds it up is screwed into the wall, as shown. The purpose of the lower slat is to give the quilt weight, which helps it hang well.

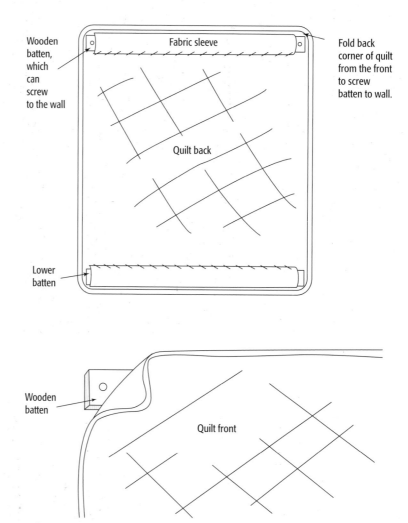

Wooden batten, which can screw to the wall

Fabric sleeve

Fold back corner of quilt from the front to screw batten to wall.

Quilt back

Lower batten

Wooden batten

Quilt front

Nottingham Reflections (detail). See full
quilt on page 108. Photo: Keith Tidball

Studio Quilts

Reflections III on page 20
illustrates large stab stitching
used for quilting. I also used
stab stitching in some of my
laminated pieces, such as
Colourbank (see page 120).
To see how I have used other
quilting techniques, look at
Cubic Log Cabin (sink stitching);
Nottingham Reflections (free-
motion quilting); *Dancing Lines*
(straight stitching). The stitching
shown in *Black and White
Bars II* on page 2 is made using
a multi-needled industrial quilting machine that I rented from a
quilting factory. Look at these to
compare different effects as you
decide which type of quilting to
try on your own quilts.

Cubic Log Cabin (detail). See full quilt on
page 77. Photo: John Coles, Cornwall

Dancing Lines (detail). See full quilt on
page 117. Photo: Keith Tidball

Painting fabric stretched onto polythene. Photo: Keith Tidball

Fabric Dyeing and Painting Workshop

CHAPTER 4

It can be very confusing to find out about dyes and paints for fabric. All products have their own trade names, and instructions and recipes are always different. Then there is the decision of whether to use natural or chemical dyes, or hot-water or cold-water dyes. In this Workshop, I will try to answer some of the many questions you are likely to have by telling you about the dyes and paints I have tried and tested over several years. You can then feel confident that the recipes included here will work. For both dyeing and painting, I will run through techniques for working with both small samples and larger lengths of fabric.

For dyeing cotton, I use *cold-water, fiber-reactive dyes*, a chemical dye type commonly known as Procion MX. The colors from fiber-reactive dyes tend to be a little chalky. Look, for example, at the colors in

Painting fabric (detail). Photo: Keith Tidball

WORKSHOP SUPPLIES—DYEING PROJECTS

- Cold-water fiber-reactive dyes, primary colors only (see supplies list on page 135)
- Several plastic measuring droppers, such as medicine dispensers, able to hold 5 to 10 ml of liquid—available from any pharmacy
- Glass rod stirring sticks for mixing the dye paste
- Plastic spoon for stirring

- Measuring cups
- A large jug that will hold 500 to 1,000 ml or 1 to 2 pints
- Mask (to be worn when handling powdered dyes)
- Rubber gloves
- Two screw-top jars to hold salt and soda solutions

- Wooden spoon to stir and lift fabrics in boiling water
- 100-ml plastic beakers for mixing dye
- Weighing scales, both regular cooking set and set for small quantities, i.e., 1–5 grams
- Salt
- Soda crystals
- Liquid laundry detergent for washing final fabric

Cubic Log Cabin on page 77. The recipes in this Workshop will not work with other types of dyes. For painting cotton, I use acrylic-based fabric paints. There are two types: ready-mixed paints and a textile medium that you mix yourself with acrylic paints. (See list of suppliers on page 135.)

DYEING COTTON FABRIC

I have dyed my own fabrics for several years. Recently, however, I moved my studio to a rural area of the Scottish Borders, which means that I am no longer on a main sewer system. I gave up dyeing, as I will never allow the used dye baths to drain and discharge into the beautiful river nearby. I have researched other ways of using chemicals to change the makeup of the dye water. I have also looked into building a filtering system. Since neither option seemed environmentally sound, I simply stopped dyeing. If you live in a town or city, your water recycling system should be able to cope with small amounts of fabric dye. If you are making large quantities of dye, contact your local environmental office for advice. Giving up dyeing felt like a drastic decision at the time, but it pushed me to explore fabric paints, and my quilts have taken on a whole new dimension.

The first two projects will show you how to dye precise colors. You will accurately measure and record ingredients so that you can repeat or match any color you make. The three projects that follow these allow a more relaxed, random approach, with less rigorous measuring and results that can surprise and delight.

CHOOSING FABRICS AND PREPARING TO DYE

Cold-water, fiber-reactive dyes are ideal for 100-percent-cotton fabric. They also work well with silks, although the resulting colors tend to be lighter. Avoid synthetic fibers, as the dye will not take. Check fabric labels—fabric that is "crease resistant" or permanent press—as they may be resin coated, and dye will not penetrate it.

All the projects are designed for the home or studio. In each, we will follow roughly the same dyeing process.

1. Boil the fabric to remove any nonpermanent dressing, such as sizing.
2. Prepare a dye bath of water plus the dye solution.
3. Add salt solution to drive the dye into the fibers.
4. Add soda solution to fix the dye.
5. After dyeing, wash the fabric in very hot, soapy water.
6. Rinse until the water is clear and dry.

This process should be sufficient to make the fabric completely fast. If, with very intense colors, you find it difficult to rinse the water clear, you may need to boil the fabric, then rinse again. This is rarely necessary.

Additional Supplies

See Workshop Supplies on page 37.
- A few 6" to 7" (15 cm to 18 cm) bowls: plastic, enamel, or stainless steel
- Saucepan for boiling samples before dyeing
- Thin cardboard and stapler to make color recording
- Several cotton samples, 4" × 8" (10 cm × 20 cm), weighing approximately 1/10 oz (3.5 g)

Project 12 | **Dyeing Small Samples in Precise Colors**

This dyeing method takes a little time and a lot of precision, but has some clear advantages. You can easily repeat any color you make onto larger pieces of fabric. You can dye to match specific colors. Over time, you can build a color library, keeping swatches of the fabric with the recorded recipes so that you can repeat the colors any time you choose.

Before you begin dyeing, mix up these three solutions:

- A 3-percent-dye solution (3 g dye to 100 ml water). This gives average color saturation. If you prefer a pastel shade, make a 1-percent-dye solution. Place the dye powder in a beaker and slowly add a little cold water. Stir until all the lumps dissolve and a smooth paste is formed. This process is known as *pasting up*. Slowly add warm-hot water (not boiling water), making the quantity up to 100 ml. This dye solution will have a shelf life of three days.
- A 25-percent-salt solution (25 g salt to 100 ml boiling water). Stir until salt is dissolved. Store in a screw-top jar. This solution will keep indefinitely.
- A 20-percent-soda solution (20 g soda to 100 ml boiling water). Stir until soda is dissolved. Store in a screw-top jar. This solution will keep indefinitely.

You are now ready to dye a fabric sample.

1. Boil fabric samples to remove any dressing.
2. Put 200 ml water in a bowl.
3. Add required amount of dye solution—1 ml will give a pastel shade; 60 ml gives a strong color. Record quantity used. Stir well.
4. Place wet fabric in dye bath and leave to soak for 5 to 10 minutes. Remove.
5. Add 7 ml (twice weight of fabric) salt solution to dye bath. Stir well.
6. Return fabric to dye bath. Stir well. Leave for 15 minutes, stirring frequently. Remove.
7. Add 3.5 ml (same as weight of fabric) soda solution to dye bath. Stir.
8. Return fabric to dye bath. Let stand for at least 1 hour and no more than 4 hours. Stir every 15 minutes. Remove fabric and rinse in clear water.
9. Wash the fabric in very hot water and a little liquid detergent for 5 minutes. Rinse until water is clear.
10. Dry out of direct heat or sunlight. Staple a record of dye quantities used to the sample.

Project 13 | Dyeing Large Amounts of Fabric in Precise Colors

Once you have experimented with dyeing small samples, you can repeat any of the colors you have created in quantities large enough for complete quilts. I recommend dyeing no more than 4 yards (3½ meters) at a time. First you need to figure out how many times larger your fabric is than the samples we made in the previous project. Then, simply multiply the dye solution accordingly. For example, 1⅛ yards (1 m) of fabric is approximately 40 times larger than the 4" × 8" (10 cm × 20 cm) sample. Multiply the original sample dye quantities by 40 to obtain the correct amount. There is no need to be as meticulous with the salt solution and soda solution quantities. You can use the following amounts and dissolve them in enough boiling water to make the grains and crystals disappear. For 1⅛ yards (1 m) of fabric, you will need 2½ oz (75 g) of salt and 1 oz (25 g) of soda. For 1 lb (500 g) of fabric, or 3½ yards (3 m), you will need 8 oz (225 g) of salt and 3 oz (75 g) of soda. There is no need to measure specific quantities of water—just make sure you have enough to immerse the fabric and to move it freely in the dye bath.

1. Cut the required length of white cotton fabric. Boil to remove any dressing.
2. Rinse in cold water and soak.
3. Prepare the dye bath, measuring required amounts of dye solution and water as described above. Mix well in plastic bucket or garbage can or washing machine.

To Make a Sample Color Card
Cut a 1½" (4 cm) strip off the width of your sample. Fold it in half and staple it to an index card. Record the dye amounts for future reference. Record blues on one card, reds on another, and so forth to build a card library. Once you have collected several swatches, you can even guess formulas by comparing previously dyed colors.

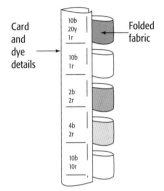

Card and dye details → | Folded fabric

10b
20y
1r

10b
1r

2b
2r

4b
2r

10b
10r

Additional Supplies
See Workshop Supplies on page 37.
- Screw-top bottles for mixing dye.
- Plastic funnel.
- Plastic bucket or garbage can, depending upon fabric quantity. An old-style top-loading washing machine—the type that you can simply turn on and off without going through different wash cycles—is ideal for dyeing 4-yard (3.5-m) lengths.

With this method you can achieve an even color over the whole length of fabric. To ensure this happens:

- Make sure the fabric has plenty of room to move around in the water.
- Always remove fabric from dye bath when adding solutions.
- Keep fabric moving—especially in the first half hour after adding the salt solution.
- Press fabric before it is completely dry to iron out all creases.
- Do not fold fabric until it is completely dry and aired out.

4. Immerse wet fabric and soak for five minutes. Remove.
5. Mix required amount of salt into a solution. Add to dye bath. Stir well.
6. Return fabric to dye bath. Stir frequently over next 30 minutes to allow the dye to react with the fibers, unraveling twisted fabric if necessary. Remove.
7. Mix required amount of soda solution. Add to dye bath. Stir well.
8. Return fabric to dye bath and immerse for 1 to 4 hours, stirring every 15 minutes. Remove and rinse in water.
9. Wash fabric thoroughly in very hot water (as hot as your hands can bear) with a little liquid detergent. Rinse until water is clear.
10. Dry out of direct heat or sunlight. Press.

Additional Supplies

See Workshop Supplies on page 37.
- Plastic bucket
- Large saucepan for boiling fabric
- Teaspoons

Project 14 | **Random Dyeing**

If you do not have the patience to measure out the exact quantities required for the first two projects, this method is for you. The results are difficult to predict—but you may accidentally hit on some colors you love! Before you begin dyeing, mix up these three solutions to dye 1⅛ yards (1 m) fabric:

- Dye solution. Use any amount up to 2 teaspoons of dye powder. Paste up the dye by adding a little cold water and mixing well, then some warm-hot water.
- Salt solution. Use 3 oz (75 g) of salt for dye quantities up to 1 teaspoon. Use 6 oz (150 g) if dye quantity is between 1 and 2 teaspoons.
- Soda solution. Use 1 oz (25 g) of soda crystals and stir to dissolve in boiling water.

1. Boil fabric to remove any dressing.
2. Rinse in cold water and soak in a bucket for five minutes. Make sure there is enough water for fabric to move freely. Remove the fabric.
3. Add dye solution. Stir well.
4. Immerse wet fabric and soak for 10 minutes. Remove.
5. Add salt solution to dye bath. Stir well.
6. Return fabric to dye bath. Stir frequently over next 30 minutes. Remove.
7. Add soda solution to dye bath. Stir well.
8. Return fabric to dye bath and allow to stand for 1 hour, stirring every 15 minutes. Remove and rinse in water.
9. Wash fabric in very hot water with a little liquid detergent. Rinse until water is clear.
10. Dry out of direct heat or sunlight. Press.

Overdyeing

With each of the methods we've used so far, you will not "see" your fabric color until the fabric is dry. Sometimes the final color will be lighter than you intended, sometimes darker. If you are not satisfied, you can overdye the fabric by repeating the process. You can also overdye commercial fabrics, provided they are 100-percent cotton and without permanent dressing.

FABRIC PAINTING

The projects below will familiarize you with fabric paints and painting techniques, with both small and large samples. As with dyes, there are several types of paint on the market. I use two types of acrylic-based paints. (See list of suppliers on page 135.) The first is a ready-mixed screen and fabric paint available in several colors; the other is a colorless textile medium base that can be mixed with acrylic paints. The medium and paint are mixed in equal quantities. Both paints are water-based and can be thinned down with water. All brushes and equipment can be washed with soap and water. Using the textile medium tends to be a little less expensive, but can add an unpleasant thickness to the fabric when it is used fairly thickly. Both products are very versatile and offer the quiltmaker great control in the hand coloring of fabrics.

STRETCHING FABRIC FOR PAINTING

Always stretch your fabric before painting to keep it flat and taut while applying the paint. There are three ways to do this:

- Using masking tape, stretch the fabric on polythene plastic sheeting attached to the floor or a board. Smooth the fabric out and place tape around all edges.
- Use a quilting or embroidery hoop. Here, you are limited to painting within the 14" (36 cm) circle of stretched fabric. However, you can move the hoop around a larger piece of fabric, if required.
- Use a wooden rectangle or square frame. Pin the fabric onto this with tacks or staples.

Ready-mixed fabric paints come with an "extender medium" that makes the paint more transparent without watering it down, thus keeping the color's intensity. It also keeps the paint consistency the same—if you prefer this—and gives it a transparent quality. For example, if you were to paint a large brush stroke, allow it to dry, then paint another on top using a different color, you would be able to see layers of color. If you use water only to thin down the paint, you will get a more opaque color. To achieve an intense, even color, try painting two or three layers, allowing the paint to dry between layers.

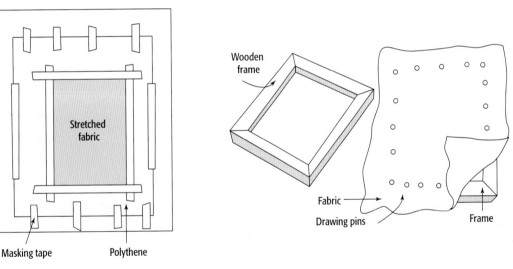

Stretched fabric

Masking tape   Polythene

Wooden frame

Fabric

Drawing pins   Frame

WORKSHOP SUPPLIES—FABRIC PAINTING PROJECTS

- Cotton fabric, prewashed and ironed
- Masking tape
- Plastic sheeting
- Frame for stretching fabric (optional)

- Good selection of paintbrushes, including household paintbrushes, stiff-bristle brushes, and stencil brushes
- Bowls or plates for mixing colors

- Acrylic fabric paints, primary colors plus black and white (see supplies list on page 135)

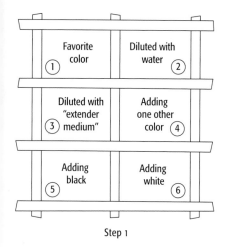

Favorite color ①	Diluted with water ②
Diluted with "extender medium" ③	Adding one other color ④
Adding black ⑤	Adding white ⑥

Step 1

Project 15 | **Painting Small Samples**

This project will introduce you to fabric painting, giving you a feel for how the paints handle.

1. Stretch a 12" (30 cm) square of fabric. Divide the fabric into six equal rectangles using masking tape.
2. Mix a teaspoon of your favorite color, adding a little water to thin it down slightly. Paint onto the first rectangle. Set the paint aside.
3. For the second rectangle, dilute a portion of the paint to make a thin wash.
4. For the third rectangle, mix some of the original mixed paint with an equal amount of extender medium.
5. For the fourth rectangle, add one other color to a portion of the original mixed paint.
6. For the fifth rectangle, add black to a portion of the original mixed paint.
7. For the last rectangle, add white to a portion of the original mixed paint.
8. Allow the paint to dry thoroughly. Remove from stretched position and remove all masking tape. Hang to dry for a further 24 hours.
9. Press on the reverse of the fabric with a hot iron for about 5 minutes per 12" × 12" (30 cm × 30 cm) of fabric. Do this in a well-ventilated space, as some fumes will come off the fabric.
10. Wash the fabric in hot water using a little liquid detergent. Rinse, dry, and press.

Project 16 | **Mixing Colors**

This project will give you the experience of mixing colors to match and will help you gain confidence with the paints.

1. Stretch a 12" (30 cm) square of fabric. Divide the fabric into six equal rectangles using masking tape. (See previous project.)
2. Choose two objects in your room or studio in colors you like. Make three attempts to match the exact color of each, thereby filling all six rectangles. (Allow each rectangle to dry before beginning the next so that you can judge the final color.)
3. Allow the paint to dry thoroughly. Remove from stretched position and remove all masking tape. Hang to dry for a further 24 hours.
4. Press on the reverse of the fabric with a hot iron for about 5 minutes per 12" × 12" (30 cm × 30 cm) of fabric.
5. Wash the fabric in hot water using a little liquid detergent. Rinse, dry, and press.

Project 17 | **Color Washes**

Here, you can experience handling thinner paint, which can easily cover large areas of fabric.

1. Stretch a 16" × 20" (40 cm × 50 cm) piece of fabric.
2. Paint over the whole fabric with clear water, using a large brush.
3. Mix two favorite colors to a fairly liquid state. Color half the fabric in the first color and half in the second color. Leave to dry thoroughly. The colors will blend into each other and form a beautiful wash.
4. Remove from stretched position and remove all masking tape. Hang to dry for a further 24 hours.
5. Press on the reverse of the fabric with a hot iron for about 5 minutes per 12" × 12" (30 cm × 30 cm) of fabric.
6. Wash the fabric in hot water with a little liquid detergent. Rinse, dry, and press.

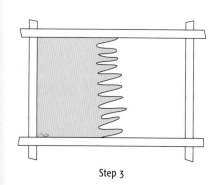

Step 3

OTHER FABRIC PAINT TECHNIQUES

As you experiment, you will discover that acrylic paints are extremely versatile, and there are many, many ways in which you can use them to add excitement to fabrics you will use in your quilts. *Colour Study I*, on page 64, is an example of one quilt in which I used painted fabrics. Here are a few ideas you may enjoy.

- Make a stencil by cutting a shape out of thin cardboard. Mix the paint to a fairly thick consistency. Place the cardboard with shape cut out on the fabric. Using a stencil brush, apply an even layer of paint to the fabric, filling in the outlined shape of the stencil. The shape can be repeated to form a pattern by allowing this first painted area to dry and then repositioning the stencil and repeating the process.
- Create stripes across the fabric by blocking out strips with masking tape before painting.
- Gather, tie, or stitch the fabric, then apply paint roughly over the top surface. Allow to dry, then remove the stitching. This method offers an effect similar to tie-dyeing.
- Use a household paint roller to apply paint in multiple directions over the fabric.
- Crush a piece of paper or fabric and dip it in paint. Apply it to a piece of stretched fabric, blotting random patterns onto the fabric.
- Use sponges to dab paint onto the fabric, creating texture or making patterns.
- Use rubber stamps or potato cuts. Patterns or textured shapes can be cut into either of these and used to print onto fabric.

Once you start working with fabric paints, you will find new ways of your own to apply color, shape, and texture to your fabrics. This is not only very enjoyable but can make your quilts even more original. It is very rewarding to start from scratch in this way, and working directly with an open, limitless color range is a wonderful experience.

Studio Quilt

The detail of *Colourbank* shown here is a very obvious use of my painted fabrics. I have deliberately matched the painted cloth to the color of the petals to make them merge together. I have also used the painted cloth in a more subtle way in such pieces as *Colour Study I* and *Angela's Garden III*. Today, I am still using fabrics that I dyed years ago in such works as *Tone*, shown on page xviii. You'll also see them in earlier quilts such as *Cubic Log Cabin* on page 77 and *Liquorice Allsorts* on page 72.

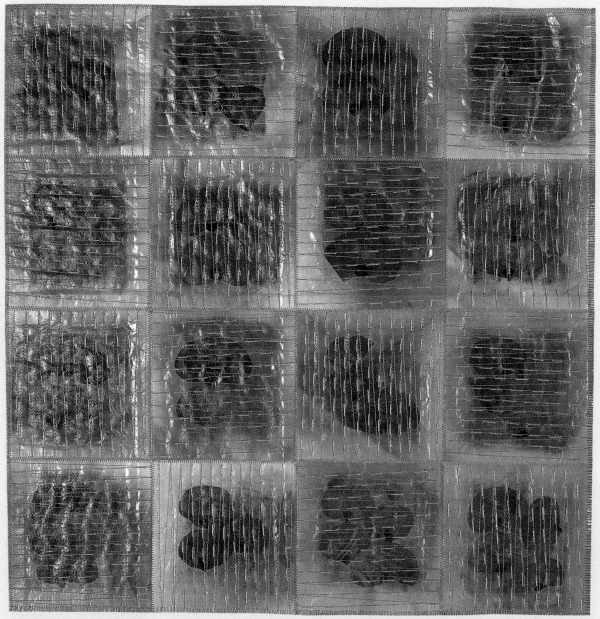

Colourbank (detail). See full quilt on page 120. Photo: Keith Tidball

Meet Pauline Burbidge
An Interview with Penny McMorris

Pauline and Charlie.

In the Studio

Penny McMorris: The Scottish Border country where you now live has really had an impact on your work. Can you describe what you went through to create your present home and studio?

Pauline Burbidge: My husband, Charlie, and I bought Allanbank Mill Steading at the end of 1993. It consisted of a group of farm buildings with no house. The two main buildings were the stables with hayloft and the granary and byre (cowshed). The granary was the only really dry place, so we made this our temporary home, as we began remodeling the buildings.

We often think back to those times of not having heating or water in our living space. It was a real challenge, and we quite enjoyed the inventiveness of living like this—back to basics. The outside tap was often frozen over, and so, too, was last night's tea, in the bottom of the mug. We did have electricity. So our great luxury was an electric blanket! But we often had to go to bed at 8:30 at night in order to simply keep warm.

Both Charlie and I gave up working on our artwork for the whole year it took us to convert our farm buildings to living and studio spaces. Charlie did half the construction work himself, helped initially by a team of builders who reroofed the buildings and got the basic shell of the house in order. In the meantime, I was teaching as many workshops as I could, trying to earn as much as possible to pay for living expenses and building supplies.

Our conversion started in October of 1993 and went through the winter. We finally moved into the house space, part of the former stable and hayloft, the following August. It took time for us to settle into our studio spaces, and it proved much harder to get back to doing our artwork than we had imagined. It was strange, really, when I first began working, because my studio space (formerly the hayloft) was new and orderly, yet below me our house was still stables, with no windows fitted and gales blowing through.

By August 1994 we had finished our living spaces, and also the granary, which became Charlie's studio. The other buildings have great potential, but at the moment we just use them roughly as they are. With a bit of cleaning up and white paint, they make good exhibition spaces.

Pauline at Allanbank.
Photo: Keith Tidball

Allanbank before renovations, 1993. Photo: Pauline Burbidge

Construction work in the living room and kitchen, 1993. Photo: Pauline Burbidge

We now hold an Open Studio Exhibition once a year (see photographs on pages xv and xvi). We open up for three days in August and display our work around the steading in all the buildings and our studios. It's important for us to show our work here, where we live, in this environment. And it's a marker point in the year for us. We also enjoy having so many visitors.

Every September I hold more annual events and run workshops in the village hall in Allanton—a weekend course for more advanced students as well as two Saturday workshops. Since these classes are immediately after our Open Studio, we usually still have work on display for my students to see.

Penny McMorris: How would you describe your "typical working day?"

Pauline Burbidge: I rise early. After breakfast I go for a quick half-hour walk and think about my day's work. If I'm lucky, I'll be going straight into the studio (my favorite type of day!). More probably, I will have to spend the morning completing office work.

On studio days, I spend the morning working on fabric collage work, or maybe outside taking photos. If it's office work, I make phone calls, write letters, or plan workshops.

Each afternoon, I try and work on the more mundane side of my work—the craft work—stitching by hand or machine for example. This can be a bit like meditation for me.

If I don't have an urgent deadline, I will spend an hour in the garden in late afternoon. Then we eat about six o'clock and usually work for another two hours into the evening.

Penny McMorris: How much of the year do you spend in the studio versus teaching?

Pauline Burbidge: This is a difficult question, as I may spend a period of six months researching visual material,

taking photos mainly. Then this may set me up with imagery to work with over the next eighteen months.

In two years, for example, year one might equal six months collecting photos, six months making samples, and perhaps making three small pieces. In year two I might make three or four smaller works, and also produce two large quilts. So in two years I would have made two large quilts and perhaps six smaller works. This would be a good output for me. I have to work like this to build up to the large works.

About half my time is spent teaching workshops. Of course, I have a lot of work to do preparing my workshops and organizing exhibitions, and so on, so in reality I would say that probably leaves only about 40 percent of my time for studio work.

I very much like to teach, and I really enjoy meeting everyone, both students and other teachers. These days I am trying to fit my teaching into blocks of one or two weeks, and am not accepting single days or even weekends, as they are too disruptive of my studio time. A one-day workshop can end up taking four days of my time—preparing/traveling/ teaching/traveling and thinking over the class and the students I've met.

Penny McMorris: Tell us about your studio and the equipment you use.

Pauline Burbidge: I have good light, large tables and an ironing table, and wall space covered with soft board, so that I can construct my work on this surface.

The sewing machine that I use is a single-needle Bernina. In the past, I have used some industrial, multi-needled, quilting machines to quilt my work. But I had to rent these and use them in a factory. I do not own one. The industrial machines forced me to finish several tops at a time, then quilt them all. These days I prefer to start and finish one quilt at a time.

Pauline's main studio, Allanbank. Photo: Keith Tidball

Experience

Penny McMorris: How important do you feel it is to enter quilt shows when you're getting started?

Pauline Burbidge: It seems very important to enter mixed exhibitions: some quilt shows and some shows open to all kinds of work. It is a good way of networking, meeting other artists, and comparing notes on all sorts of things, such as where else they exhibit.

Exhibiting your work has all sorts of benefits. For example, it's a time to reassess your work, to think of future developments, to sell work, to get feedback from others, to make contact with critics and gallery organizers as well as other artists, to get your work in print, on postcards, or in catalogs.

Penny McMorris: In the U.S., there currently seem to be a never-ending series of classes teaching endless numbers of techniques. What's your take on this? Do you think it's necessary to take classes, or can one still just learn on their own?

Pauline Burbidge: I feel quilt-makers could benefit from getting information from a much

broader textile or art and design field. I hope many of the design projects in this book will happily relate to general surface pattern design students, as well as quiltmakers—crossovers in different areas are important.

There are many derivative quilts being made. It would be helpful to look wider into other art and design areas. Good slide lectures can be very valuable, as can workshops that really go thoroughly into techniques (e.g., fabric dyeing) or into general art and design projects.

Most quiltmakers who (in my opinion) are producing top-rate work have usually had some sort of art and design education. But occasionally someone self-taught produces the most original material.

What a difficult subject art is to teach! Often in the U.K. certain "house styles" can be spotted in graduate work from various different colleges. This seems slightly unavoidable, as the students will be exposed to the same lectures, exhibition studies, etc. And teachers are, of course, attracted to certain types of work and not others.

Yet teachers should really concentrate on drawing out the individual student's character, beliefs, color choices, and so on. As art or quilting students, everyone should be encouraged to think differently. Occasionally this may take the form of not going through an organized program. But learning on your own is a lonely business. You must find one or two people who are sympathetic to your attempts at creative expression and who try to understand your aims. And so here we go full circle—for you are most likely to find these people in a course connected with your art.

Water Reflections, Paxton Pond. Photo: Pauline Burbidge

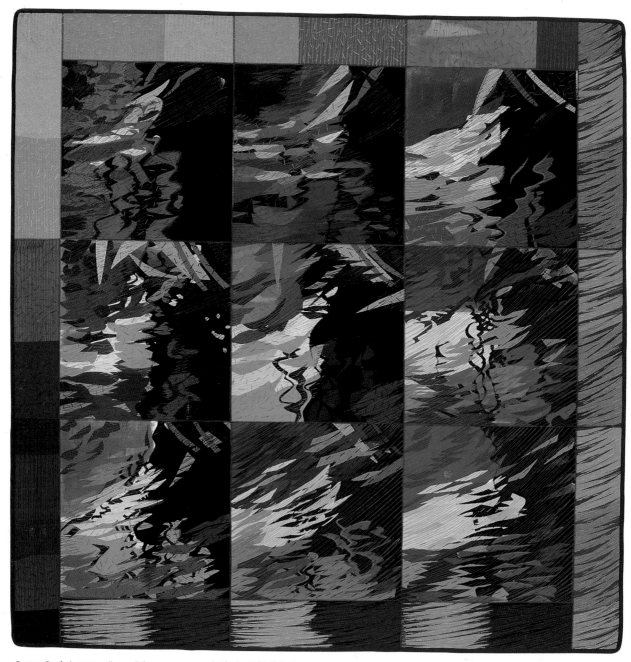

Paxton Study I, 1997, 50″ × 50″ (127 cm × 127 cm). Photo: Keith Tidball

Penny McMorris: *You're firmly connected to the quilting world in Great Britain as undoubtedly its best-known artist/quiltmaker. Yet you're also well known outside the quilt world. Have you made a concerted effort to keep a foot in both the quilt and the craft/art camps for a reason?*

Pauline Burbidge: Yes. The quilting world has connected me with all sorts of exhibitions, workshop events, and conferences worldwide, which has given me a great opportunity to visit countries I would otherwise never have been able to see.

The art/craft arena has given me occasional grant support and access to the best gallery spaces, mainly in the U.K. and occasionally abroad. It feels very important to show my work in the best possible spaces.

I feel both worlds are important. They attract different people, and in order to sell one quilt I have to show thousands of people the work. Therefore it feels necessary and sensible to keep my options open in both camps.

Penny McMorris: *You've done many quilts on commission. Can you tell someone who has never made a quilt on commission how this works? How do you get a commission? And how do you try to ensure that the final quilt satisfies both you and the consignor?*

Pauline Burbidge: I actually don't seek out commissions very often, for two main reasons: first, because I usually like to follow my own themes in my work; second, because the ideas put forward for themes are usually inappropriate.

I never make two pieces of work alike. I prefer to make work on my own and try to sell it through exhibitions. So if a client sees a piece of work in an exhibition, and it is sold, I cannot make an identical piece, and I may not even be able to make a piece in the same series if it is not my current theme.

If someone is keen to commission work, I ask them to keep in touch with my work developments over the next year or so. If possible, they should visit our annual Open Studio Exhibition. They may decide to buy one of my older quilts, or become interested in my current work.

I need to know if the commissioned work is to go into a particular space or fill a certain spot in a collection. I also need to know their budget, so I can suggest what size piece they would get for their money. And so the conversation begins to build.

Some people are too impatient. They want a piece instantly. In this case it's best for them to buy a completed quilt. I cannot force the pace of the work, or have any too fixed or rigid ideas at the beginning of a work. If I do, I can't make the most creative quilt. So people have to trust my current work, my reputation, and probably a rough sketch and samples. I can no longer work from a very detailed, finished design drawing as I used to. I find it doesn't allow me to produce my most creatively free, spiritual, and best work.

Pauline in her Nottingham studio, 1991. Photo: Keith Tidball

There can easily be misinterpretations and misunderstandings with commissions. If someone hears that you make textile wall hangings, for example, they create their own mental picture. Whereas you, the artist, are convinced that they are visualizing something else. So there must be a great deal of communication before you begin to work, so that you both understand one another. Once an understanding is reached, you need to draw up a written contract stating:

1. Visual theme—submit reference material, drawings, collages, photos, etc.
2. Budget for the work
3. Dates when payments are due—perhaps in two or three payments
4. Dates when work will be completed and delivered

If your timetable dates start shifting backwards, let the client know. Keep communicating!

Penny McMorris: *You began making quilts back before quilting was the booming industry of today. Can you imagine yourself just starting out now? How would you feel about all of the influences, shows, books that are so much a part of today's quilting?*

Pauline Burbidge: I know that I would feel that it was a very commercial world, which would probably put me off doing it! I would seek out something else that was far more obscure. I think this is the artist in me who wants to be doing something different than the mainstream.

When I started quiltmaking, I was working in isolation. It really felt like the right thing to have found. I related so much to using and creating with fabric. I tucked myself away in solitude to produce work and then, as a contrast, periodically exhibited my work or taught workshops. I enjoyed mixing with fellow enthusiasts and it helped build up my self-confidence.

Paxton Study I (detail). Photo: Keith Tidball

Pauline in her Nottingham studio, 1991. Photo: Keith Tidball

Penny McMorris: *You've never used many printed fabrics in your work—you're known for using solids. Why is that?*

Pauline Burbidge: Early on, when I was making pieced images, I was keen to use plain fabrics in order to show the full value of the pieced images. I felt that if I were to use floral prints, some of the boldness of the images would be lost.

Penny McMorris: *When did you begin hand-dyeing fabric, and are you still doing this?*

Pauline Burbidge: I used to hand-dye my fabric when I lived in Nottingham [England]. Back then, I dyed about a quarter of the fabrics I used. Now I do not dye fabric at all— but I paint cloth with fabric paint instead. I changed processes because we live out in the countryside and our drains are not connected to main drainage. Therefore if I were to dye cloth, the bathful of colored water would go straight into the river untreated!

Penny McMorris: *You're now using a radically unusual "fabric" in your quilts. Tell us about the plastic you're using and how you began using it.*

Pauline Burbidge: This started with one of my quilts called *Whiteadder* where I wanted to trap loose fabric down under a transparent layer. None of the fabrics I could find were completely transparent. So I used plastic—the type that you might cover a book with. Then I stitched on top of the plastic. Later, I found a lamination plastic specially made for

fabric, so I am using this on my color study pieces. I trap dried flower petals between the fabric and laminating plastic. I iron it for a few seconds on the back of the fabric to make it permanently bond to the cloth.

Penny McMorris: *Life is a matter of making choices. What choices did you make in order to further your artistic career?*

Pauline Burbidge: The biggest one has been never to compromise my work for commercial reasons. I would never change the work in order to sell it. I know this is the most difficult route, but for me it's the only pure way of making art. It's something a businessperson cannot understand: I will not change my "product" to fit a market. Therefore I have had to earn money sometimes doing other things to support my work—pattern cutting in my early years; teaching workshops now.

I try to live fairly basically—as much as is possible today. Luckily, my husband, Charlie, agrees with this philosophy, as he is an artist too. We do not have children to support, which has been a conscious decision by both of us separately (earlier in our lives) in order to allow us to concentrate and spend time making artwork.

Penny McMorris: *You are self-supporting in a country with relatively few quilt collectors or other patrons. What advice do you have for quiltmakers who would like to "quit their day job" and support themselves by making quilts?*

Pauline Burbidge: Get a part-time job—skilled, if possible —to support your quiltmaking work.

Inspirations and Influences

Penny McMorris: Where do you look for ideas and inspiration?

Pauline Burbidge: It is a difficult thing to put into words. I feel my work is about the celebration of color, shade, form, pattern, and texture. When I'm involved in making a quilt, quite often I am in a world which doesn't relate to the written or spoken word much. I am in a sort of vacuum which relates to passions, decisions, and gut reactions about the work. I am happy to wallow in this suspended space—it is a very special place for me, but it often sounds silly and pretentious to try and talk about it!

My current work reflects my surroundings. I love to go out and photograph the countryside. At the moment I am very intrigued by water reflections and continue to work on this theme. The way the images move and disperse and re-form again, according to the wind, tides, and activity on the water surface all fascinate me.

Also, I am collecting material around me, such as flower petals and leaves, pressing them, and laminating them to fabric. These become color studies. By observing the color, this heightened color awareness then feeds into my water reflections work. One work leads into another.

Penny McMorris: Do you believe someone can really become an artist, or develop a style of their own, if they work hard enough at it? Or do you believe being artistic is a talent you're born with?

Pauline Burbidge: A bit of both! But the word *determination* comes in here. If you have a lot of determination, and believe in yourself and your work, then this goes a long way! You definitely have to work hard at it and occasionally, when you get a high point or a buzz from the work you're making, this makes it all worthwhile. This also could be thought of as the talent bit, I think. It's sort of a higher plane.

Penny McMorris: Your husband is also an artist. Do you influence each other's work?

Pauline Burbidge: I'm sure we do influence each other's work, but we try not to. Charlie is a sculptor. We share a belief in the importance of our own work, and of not wanting to compromise our work for commercial reasons, which seems very important. But while we help each other out with office-work type decisions often, we try to only comment on work in progress when invited. It feels necessary not to simply allow comments to come out at any time, as they may influence the process of the work.

Whiteadder, 1995, 33" × 33" (83 cm × 83 cm). Photo: Keith Tidball

Whiteadder River. Photo: Pauline Burbidge

"Joining Forces" Exhibition at the Angle Row Gallery, Nottingham, 1993. A joint show with work by
Pauline Burbidge and Charles Poulsen. Photo: Keith Tidball

Penny McMorris: *Do you find the stimulation of being
around other artists brings new ideas to your work?*

Pauline Burbidge: Contact with other serious artists does
seem very important. I don't feel that I am particularly influenced by their work, but there is a sort of silent understanding which is comforting, somehow knowing that we are all
obsessed with our own work! We don't have to start from
scratch, explaining what it is we are trying to do.

Living where we do, in the rural area of the Scottish
Borders where the population is scarce, it has taken us a
while to find a network of artists whose works we respect.
But now, after five years of living here, this network is beginning to develop. We encourage our artist friends to come to
our annual Open Studio, and now four or five of them are
beginning to run similar annual promotional events.

Penny McMorris: *Speaking of contacts with other artists, I
know some have come and stayed in your "caravan." Tell me
about it.*

Pauline Burbidge: Our caravan [trailer] is our guest room
(in summer months only!). We bought it secondhand and
decided to paint it up. Outside it's purple and yellow
stripes—inside cream with large purple dots. Charlie and I
sometimes go "on holiday" ourselves in it—just hop over the

wall in our own garden. We have had many friends stay,
including Michael and Judy James. Michael has been
extremely supportive over the years in the way that he's
shown work of mine in exhibitions and written about me.
We really enjoyed their visit. Afterwards Michael based a
quilt on their visit, entitled *Allanbank Caravan.*

The Stripey Caravan, Allanbank. Photo: Pauline Burbidge

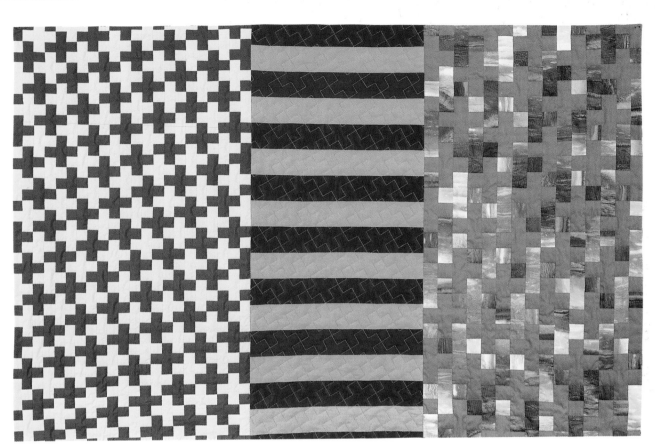

Allanbank Caravan, 1997, by Michael James, 39" × 69½" (99 cm × 176 cm). Photo: David Caras

Penny McMorris: *How have you managed not to be influenced by other quiltmakers?*

Pauline Burbidge: It doesn't seem to be a problem at all. I appreciate the work of other quiltmakers, without looking toward their work for ideas. I look at other things for inspiration and don't feel that making quilts is a competitive thing at all. Everyone is developing their own visual language.

Penny McMorris: *So what's next for you?*

Pauline Burbidge: I really feel as though I want to concentrate my efforts on creating a body of work and exhibiting it in one- or two-person shows—having a big exhibition every three or four years, cutting out all group shows altogether. That's what really feels right for me now.

Penny McMorris is an art consultant specializing in contemporary quilts. She served as the corporate art curator for Owens Corning Corporation for 20 years. McMorris coauthored The Art Quilt, *the first book on contemporary quiltmakers. She has hosted 36 PBS television programs on quilting. She is founder and vice president of the quilt design software firm the Electric Quilt Company.*

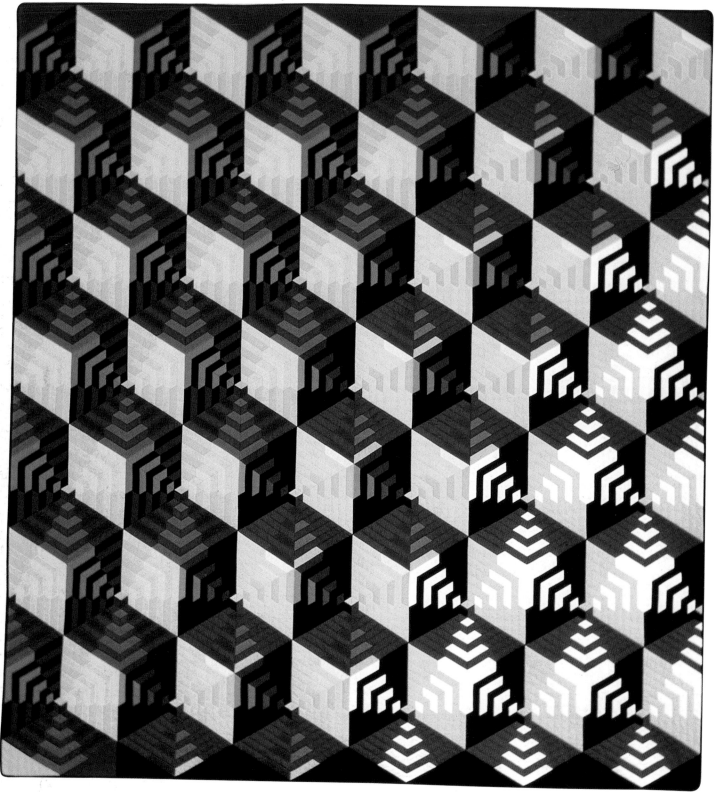

Cubic Pyramid, 1982, 86½" × 80" (220 cm × 203 cm). Photo: John Coles, Cornwall

DESIGN

Once you become adept with the techniques we covered in Part One, you are ready to turn your thoughts to design. To help you gain confidence, the Workshops in Part Two are structured into specific design projects that, as you will see, serve a dual purpose. They act as examples of essential design processes and are a starting point for developing your own design ideas. Rather than learning how to make different types of quilts, which is the approach of most quiltmaking books, you will begin developing your own "visual language." This will take you much further as a quiltmaker and will be of lasting value.

The Workshops in Part Two cover the creative processes that help you develop as a quiltmaker. We will look at specific construction styles, such as strip piecing, geometric three-dimensional design, and fabric collage. Workshops on color and pattern will help you broaden your vision. Through a series of samples in which you will experiment with ideas, you will experience how the design process works and be encouraged to design for yourself.

My objective is to provide some answers to a question that I am often asked by other quiltmakers, by quilt collectors, and by those who have admired my work—"Where do you get your inspiration from?" This is a very involved question to answer. It is inspiration that makes each quilt unique, an expression of its maker. It is my hope that working through the projects and beginning your own design samples will help you find your own answers and discover your own sources of inspiration.

Heron, 1981, 90" × 96" (228 cm × 243 cm). Photo: Pauline Burbidge

Strip-Piecing Workshop | CHAPTER 5

Often, technique and design overlap, and strip piecing is a perfect example. In this Workshop, we will first analyze the technique, finding out just how versatile it is, and then design around it, translating images into fabric. I devised my own method of strip piecing many years ago. I thought it would be a good technique to use for creating pictorial-type images. *Fruit Basket* (see detail on page 63) is an example. It was inspired by antique "postage stamp" quilts, where the image was made up of tiny squares. I began by designing with similar squares, then thought about using strips of fabric instead.

In the first three projects in this Workshop, I use a simple heart shape to demonstrate three methods of design that use the principles of strip piecing. These are not meant to be turned into full quilts. However, you might like one of your blocks so much that you decide to make up several blocks and turn them into a quilt. In later projects, I encourage you to develop more complex designs and also take you through some alternative, more free-form approaches to strip piecing.

Heron II (detail), 1981 (pieced), 1988 (quilted).
Photo: Keith Tidball

WORKSHOP SUPPLIES

- General drawing equipment, including a good selection of pencils, pencil sharpener, ruler, and eraser
- General sewing equipment, including sewing machine and a good selection of machine threads
- Paper and fabric scissors

- Glue stick, graph paper, thin cardboard, tracing paper, masking tape
- Colored pencils or paint
- White crayon or fabric marker
- Cutting mat, rotary cutter, safety ruler
- Iron and ironing board

- Selection of colored fabrics, 100-percent-cotton fabric, preferably plain weave, prewashed—approximately 10 colors in ¼ yd (0.25 m) lengths
- Selection of picture images—simple shapes that transfer easily into line drawings, such as plant and animal forms or silhouettes

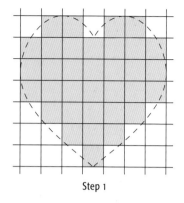

Step 1

Note: Although the design is on a small scale, you can use any size square of fabric for the finished block. Simply follow the small-scale drawing to check the layout of the squares.

Project 18 | **Designing with Squares**

One of the easiest approaches to designing your own quilt blocks is to map out shapes onto squared graph paper. This graph-paper drawing becomes the plan for your block–there is no need to draw the design full scale, as in Projects 19 and 20.

1. Begin with a simple line drawing, like the heart shown. Take a piece of graph paper and draw the heart shape onto it as shown. (The dotted line represents the simple line drawing.) Draw in a grid of squares over the line drawing. Size and position them in a way that allows you to represent the original shape in squares.

2. Recreate your shape using the square units by coloring in the squares. Remember that you can only fill in whole squares to create the solid shape. Each square on your drawing represents a square of fabric that will be pieced together to form the block.

3. Make a single square template for the finished fabric square. Draw a square the size you wish your fabric square to be onto graph paper and cut it out. Glue the graph-paper square onto thin cardboard and add seam allowances. Cut the template out.

4. Using the template, draw a few squares onto a single layer of fabric.

5. Place two more layers of fabric under the first, and using a rotary cutter cut out the squares through all layers. You will need two different colored fabrics for this design: 15 squares will be cut from a light tone for the background color and 34 from a dark tone for the heart shape.

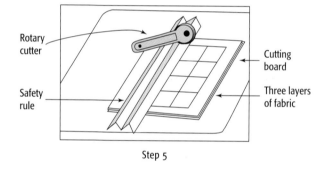

Rotary cutter

Safety rule

Cutting board

Three layers of fabric

Step 5

6. Lay the fabric squares out, using your drawing as a guide. Sew the squares together row by row. Join the finished rows together, matching seams.

Project 19 | **Designing with Right-Angled Strips**

It is easy to make the same heart design as the one in Project 18 by using strips rather than squares of fabric. By making this block you will see how simple it is to design with strips.

1. Make a strip template using graph paper and cardboard. Remember that if you want your finished strips to measure 1" (2.5 cm) wide, your template must measure 1" (2.5 cm) plus seam allowances.

2. Draw your heart shape full scale on graph paper to the size that you want the finished block to be.

3. Cut several strips, selvage to selvage, in two colored fabrics of your choice.

4. Using your full-scale graph-paper drawing as a guide, cut these into shorter strips of the appropriate length. Make sure that you add seam allowances on all sides of the strips.

5. Sew the strips together, again using your graph-paper drawing as a guide. You will end up with a block that has seam allowances on all sides, ready to piece to the next block, if you choose to do so. (See page 4.)

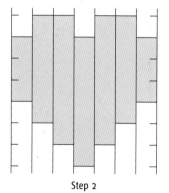

Step 2

It is a good idea to draw seam allowances around all outside edges of your graph-paper drawing so that you remember to add the outside edge seam allowance.

Project 20 | **Designing with Angled Strips**

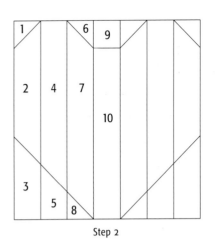

Step 2

Whereas the methods used in the last two projects produced identical heart shapes, the technique you will learn in this project will result in a less angular design. With this method, it is possible to obtain a more accurate shape, closer to the original line drawing. However, you will still be using easy, straight-edge shapes to piece your block.

1. Draw the heart shape, full scale to the size you wish your fabric block to be. Make two identical graph-paper drawings.
2. Number the required strips from 1 to 10, as shown, on both drawings.
3. Cut out the strips from one graph-paper drawing only. Paste them onto cardboard, adding seam allowances around all edges, to make templates. Set the second drawing aside for reference. You will use it to remind yourself of the order in which to sew the pieces.

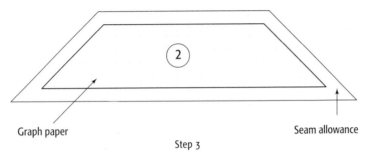

Graph paper

Seam allowance

Step 3

4. Draw around each template onto selected fabrics and cut out the shapes, ready for piecing.
5. Lay out the pieces in order, using the second graph-paper drawing as a guide. Piece each strip together, then join the strips to complete the block as shown in Project 1 on page 4.

USING STRIP-PIECING METHODS FOR MORE COMPLEX DESIGNS

Each of the three strip-piecing methods we have practiced can easily be applied to more sophisticated designs than the simple heart shape. A guiding rule is to draw the design first to a small scale, refining it until you are completely satisfied with it. Only then should you enlarge it to full size and make templates. This will save you time, paper, fabric—and frustration. One more piece of advice—keep your first designs *simple*.

Before you begin working on your own designs, read through the section that follows. Here, I describe how one of my strip-pieced designs, the *Heron* block, was created.

Creating *Heron*

Heron is a very good example of the ease with which strip piecing works. I am not suggesting that you re-create this design; rather, it is meant to illustrate the problems you may encounter as you create similar designs of your own. Once you see how *Heron* was made, you will be ready to design from your own images, using strip-piecing methods to assemble your blocks.

In creating *Heron*, I began with a very simple line drawing. I sketched it out to a small scale, at first, redrawing until I was satisfied with the lines and contours. While I sketched, I thought about how I might divide up the design for piecing.

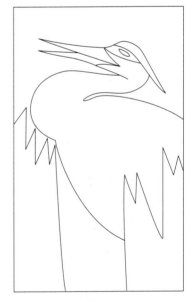

Simple line drawing

Stylized strip-pieced design

I then drew vertical lines on a piece of tracing paper, about ¼″ (0.75 cm) apart. I placed this over the line drawing and plotted in the image. Each of the lines within each strip can be set at any angle, rather than the straight vertical lines I used, according to your design needs. Think of each line as a seam line—you can change fabric with every seam. As you can see, my finished design was made up entirely of straight lines, making it easy to piece.

I then redrew the image, scaling it up to the size of my final block. (See the next section, on this page, for help on scaling up designs.) Since I was planning to piece by machine, I made sure my strips were at least 1″ (2.5 cm) wide. My design included several angled strips, so I then used the strip-piecing method we practiced in Project 20 to create templates, cut fabric, and lay out and piece the design.

The trickiest part of this design was deciding whether to divide the design into vertical or horizontal strips. This is a typical problem you are likely to run into as you begin creating your own design.

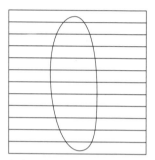

The best direction to draw the lines

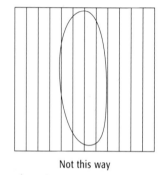

Not this way

To understand why this is important, look at the shape of the heron's beak on my drawing. By choosing vertical rules, I was able to design the beak shape into a subtle curve. If the rules had been drawn horizontally, the entire beak would likely be cut from a single strip of fabric, making it distort easily.

You can use the same piecing process to achieve greater or lesser design detail, according to the number and width of strips you draw in. (Remember, here we are going back to a design scale again.) For example, if I were to make a second *Heron* design using the same-size line drawing but with ½″ (1.5 cm) strips rather than ¼″ (0.75 cm) strips, the resulting design would be more stylized and less detailed. It would probably also be distorted in shape.

A detail from another quilt (*Fruit Basket*) that I designed with this method is shown on page 63.

SCALING UP DESIGNS

One of the most drastic transformations to a design takes place when you scale up a drawing to full-quilt size. You will find that some designs simply do not translate well from small to large. To test this out, it is always a good idea to scale up a single block or a small area of the design before you commit to it. This will give you a good idea of how the finished work will appear—and it will allow you to change direction if the original design does not scale up as well as you imagined it would.

A beauty of block quilts is the ease with which you can scale up from a design drawing. Your small-scale drawing will allow you to develop the design and see if the repeating pattern is successful. If your quilt has a block layout, you need only scale up a single block from which to make templates. You will use the same templates repeatedly to complete the quilt.

To scale up any block, use the following technique.

1. Draw a simple grid over the block design.
2. Decide on the size you wish your fabric block to be. Draw that size square onto graph paper. (The graph paper makes it easy to ensure that the shape is perfectly square.)
3. Draw a grid over this square, made up of the same number of boxes as the small-scale drawing. Label as shown.

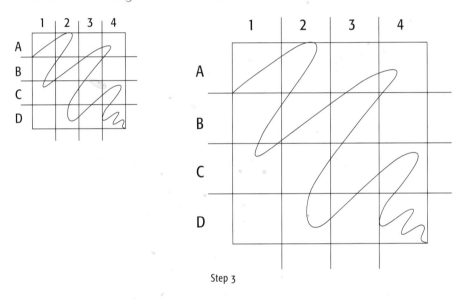

Step 3

4. Replicate the small drawing, square by square, onto the larger grid. Begin with square 1A and draw the same lines, in proportion to the larger square, in the 1A square of the larger grid. Continue until the entire image is transferred.

AN ALTERNATIVE APPROACH TO STRIP PIECING

Strip piecing is a favorite method of design for many quilters. It is systematic, unfailingly accurate, and provides predictable results. It is also, as we have seen, extremely versatile. For others, however, the exacting nature of strip piecing is maddening and, for some, limiting. If you are in search of a less precise, more free-form approach, here is another strip-piecing technique that may suit you.

Here, we still use strips of fabric but they are pieced together with far less precision than the earlier examples. Images of landscapes, like the one on the next page, are particularly well suited to this method.

Begin by selecting an image—a photograph, perhaps, or a rough sketch of a landscape, and pin it to the wall. Select colored fabrics. Using a rotary cutter, slice the fabric. Use a ruler to make sure the edges are straight. The strips need not be parallel—wedge shapes, for example, can be interesting. Next, group the strips together and

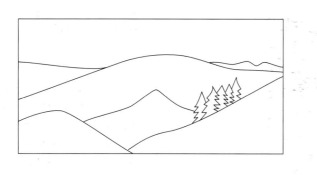

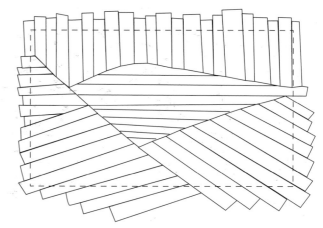

Cut back down to dotted straight line.

A simple landscape drawing adapted for strip piecing

simply begin piecing with the rough landscape image as a guide. You may need to trim the outer edges of the sections, as indeed you will also need to trim the outer edges of the finished block before you can piece it into a quilt.

This nontraditional approach to piecing is fun and spontaneous, but you have to be prepared to make mistakes. Some blocks may turn out wonderfully, while others have to be chopped up and repieced or even thrown away.

Once you have completed the projects in this Workshop, you will find that strip piecing is a remarkably simple yet wonderfully versatile quiltmaking technique. The best piece of advice I can give you when you begin strip piecing is to keep your designs simple. Once you understand and have practiced the process, allow more complex design ideas to filter through. Soon, you will be able to translate any image selected from the world around you into a strip-pieced quilt.

Studio Quilts

It is easy to see how simple line drawings can be translated into strip-pieced designs. The center of *Fruit Basket* was made with the same method as *Art Nouveau*. You can see how easy it is to create curved, flowing lines using this technique.

Fruit Basket (detail), 1979. Photo: Pauline Burbidge

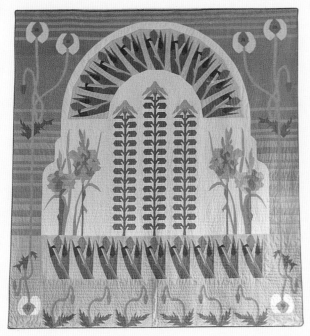

Art Nouveau Quilt, 1981, 97" × 105" (246 cm × 266 cm). Photo: Pauline Burbidge

Art Nouveau Quilt (detail). Photo: Pauline Burbidge

Colour Study I, 1997, 68" × 68" (172 cm × 172 cm). Photo: Keith Tidball

Color and Image-Collecting Workshop

This Workshop is divided into two sections: a color Workshop and my notes and ideas on collecting images for inspiration. Both topics are essential raw material for developing quilt designs.

My relationship to color as a quiltmaker and an artist is based on personal intuition and emotional response. For decades, theorists have tried to understand the elements of color by slotting colors into systematic regimens, such as the color wheel. But to me, approaches like this have the effect of flattening the emotive appeal of color. I favor a more organic approach to color, one that changes with mood and seasonal surroundings, one that is about expression and feeling and that aims to achieve spiritual balance.

Think for a moment about light blue. It is almost certain that the color you envision is not the same as that of the person next to you. While you may see a blue-green color, others may see a blue

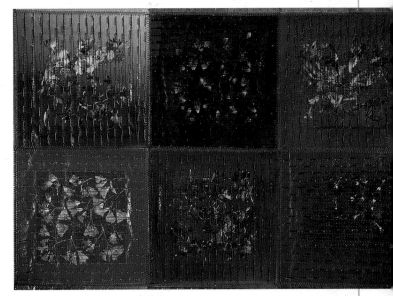

Colour Study I (detail). Photo: Keith Tidball

that veers toward purple. Your surroundings, too, affect the way you see that color: Is it bathed in sunlight? What colors surround it? How does it appear when it moves in and out of shadows? Not only do we all see color differently, we all react to it in different ways. That is why it seems to me to be an anomaly to try to teach color to others. All we can hope is to develop our own color senses and preferences and to attempt, through our quilts, to communicate those to others.

WORKSHOP SUPPLIES

- General drawing equipment, including pencils, ruler, and eraser
- Paper and fabric scissors
- Glue stick, paper glue and glue brush, newspaper, string
- White paper

- Cutting board, cutting blade
- Iron and ironing board
- Selection of colored papers, up to letter size
- Selection of 6″ (15 cm) fabric squares, backed with fusible web

- Selection of photographs, chosen for color content
- Selection of paint sample cards or paint chips, available from hardware stores
- 18 index cards or small bound notebook for making scrapbook

The projects in this Workshop will take you through various color exercises covering tone, color choice, color comparison, proportion, observation, and color grouping. The objective is to help you develop your own color language, giving you confidence in your color choices.

Project 21 | Making a Color Scrapbook

Collecting Colors

Collect a broad range of colored papers, from 6" (15 cm) square to letter size. Include both primary colors and subtle tones. Collect 6" (15 cm) fabric squares, also in a range of colors. Affix fusible web to the fabric squares to make them easier to paste into your color scrapbook by lightly ironing them into place. To increase your color range still further, collect paint chips (cards), readily available from hardware stores. The success of the Workshop depends greatly on this collection—it has to be as broad as possible. Take your time and collect as full a range of colors as you can. You can even pool your collection of colors with friends and do the projects in this Workshop together.

Creating your own scrapbook will not only heighten your awareness of color and its incredible range but will also allow you to discover your own color preferences. A color scrapbook is a quilter's most valuable companion, and it will guide your color choices in every quilt you make.

1. Punch holes in the shorter side of the index cards, so that when your color pages are complete you can tie them together into a scrapbook. You will use one side only of each card, setting color swatches slightly to the right side of the page to allow extra space for the holes and binding. Once you have completed the exercises in this Workshop, you will tie the pages together to form your color scrapbook.

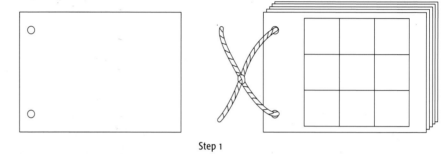

Step 1

2. Roughly cut out 1" (2.5 cm) squares of paper, fabric, and/or paint chips from your collection in black, mid-gray, and white. Paste them at the top of the first index card, with a small space between them. Next, pick any dark color, any medium color, and any light color, and put them into the appropriate columns, as shown. Repeat, filling the third row. It can help to squint at each square to help separate the tonal values. You will soon find yourself comparing colors and will be able to make fine distinctions between them. For example, you will never get a color that is as intense as the first black square. Or you'll find that a color you selected as medium in one row is better classed as dark in the next. This exercise will help you get in tune with color tone.

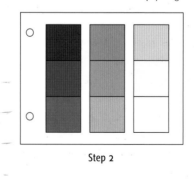

Step 2

3. What is your favorite single color? Paste a large swatch down, covering the entire index card that will form page 2 of your scrapbook.

4. On pages 3, 4, and 5, paste down three paired colors of your choice, using equal proportions of each.

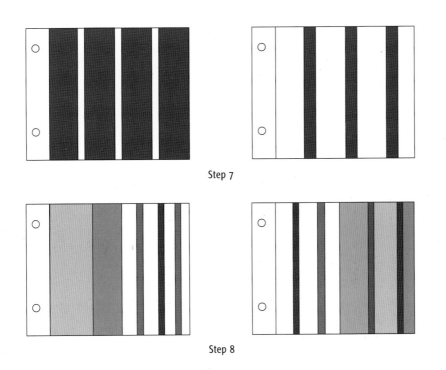

Step 7

Step 8

Selecting by Impulse
Spread your collection of colored papers, fabrics, and paint chips out on a large table. Group them together into blues, yellows, reds, etc. When choosing colors, go with your first impulse. It is the immediate, almost subconscious, emotional reaction to color that matters.

When we are asked to choose a color, we go through two stages. First, we make a quick, almost instantaneous choice. Then we enter a much more lengthy, labored process. All sorts of considerations interfere—Do I really like this color? Why do I like it? Don't I like this one just as well? I wonder what others will think of my choice? I always choose this one, so this time I'll try to be different! Before you know it, the whole thing has turned into a very complex and confusing issue. My advice is to choose quickly, keeping as close as possible to those raw, emotional responses to color that make your selections unique.

Choose colors from your paper and fabric collection. Use a glue stick to secure the paper. Peel off the backing paper and press lightly to secure the fabrics. If you are working with a group of friends or in a classroom setting, resist the temptation to check out your neighbor's color choices.

5. On pages 6, 7, and 8, paste down three pages of colors grouped in threes, again using equal amounts of each.

6. Review pages 3 through 8 and choose the two you like best. Change the surrounding colors by making a colored "window" page for each. To make a window page cover the whole page with your chosen color. Then cut a rectangular window measuring approximately 3½" × 1½" (9 cm × 4 cm) from the center of this page. Place them back in the order of pages as previously set out, this time including the "window" pages.

7. Take two favorite colors, perhaps repeating a previous choice, and change the proportions or arrangement on the next two pages, making a different color dominant on each page. Use stripes or dots, for example.

8. On the next two pages, try changing the proportions of a three-color grouping. Use different-width bands of color.

9. Choose a color that you do not like and usually avoid. Work hard to group it with other colors of your choice to come up with an arrangement that is pleasing to you. This is your next page.

10. For the next two pages choose one color that is peaceful and calm. Choose another that portrays excitement or stimulation.

11. Choose a color that you feel goes well with many other colors. Make a window page out of it. This page is to be kept loose and not tied into the scrapbook. You will be able to move it freely from page to page, masking out sections of color. Cut off the binding edge so that this page can be lodged anywhere in the scrapbook.

12. Tie the scrapbook together loosely, so that it is easy to turn the pages. Look through the pages carefully, deciding which colors and arrangements you like and which are least appealing. Gather around a table with friends who have shared this project and turn the pages of each scrapbook. Compare your different choices.

Use your scrapbook for reference each time you choose colors for a quilt. The simple exercise of creating the scrapbook will have allowed you to absorb a great deal of information on your color preferences. The projects that follow will heighten that color awareness.

Project 22 | **Color Observation**

This project will help you analyze color in the world around you, sharpening your sensitivity and increasing your awareness of personal color preferences. It will also help you look afresh at photographic images, visualizing how they may be translated into fabric.

Step 2: Study A

1. Choose a photograph that appeals to you because of its color content. Study the colors within it, separating each area of the image according to color. Try not to look at the picture or shapes within the photograph–concentrate on the colors only.

2. Collect together pieces of paper or fabric that roughly match the colors in the photograph. Trim them to 1" (2.5 cm) squares and assemble them on a sheet of white paper. Do not try to follow the proportions or the arrangements of color in the photograph; arrange them and rearrange them until the result is pleasing to you. Butt the swatches together so that no white space shows between them. Paste them down onto the paper.

3. Review both Study A and the original photograph. Repeat, this time using squares and rectangles of varying sizes instead of 1" (2.5 cm) squares. Change the proportions of color by studying the proportions in the photograph. You should find the results of this second study more pleasing than the first–it will help you understand why you were drawn to the photograph and the colors you selected in the first place. It is the *amount* of that bright blue or that red that attracts you, just as much as the color itself.

4. This time, use strips of color to build the image. Try changing the color proportion by grouping several strips of the same color together. Use a single strip in spots where you want only a small amount of color.

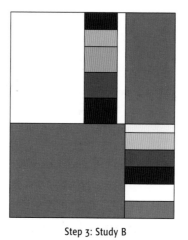

Step 3: Study B

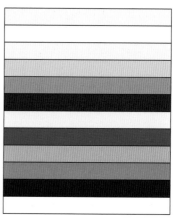

Step 4: Study C

By completing these studies, you have forced yourself to sit down and closely observe exactly which colors make up the form or image in your photograph. Once you have analyzed color and proportion in this way, you are ready to plan how to use those same colors and proportions in a quilt design. The more strongly you related to those colors as you worked through the studies, the more you will enjoy them when you work them into a quilt design.

Once you have made your color scrapbook and worked through the observation studies, you will have reference material for future projects. You will have absorbed more than you realize, simply by spending time with color. Time is the essential ingredient that allows you to become fluent and confident in color use. Each quilt project you now make will renew and strengthen your color senses.

COLLECTING IMAGES FOR INSPIRATION

The second part of this Workshop will help you develop an image collection that will spark new ideas for quilts.

Collecting images around themes that are meaningful to you is a good starting point for developing your own design style. You might take photographs yourself or clip magazine or newspaper cuttings. By pinning them to a wall in your work area, you can keep in touch with sources of inspiration that interest you. Take time to look carefully at each image and figure out why you like it. This will help you not only explore ideas but also understand more about your own visual likes and dislikes.

I have found it particularly helpful to be able to categorize possible sources of inspiration and thereby organize the images I collect. Your ideas may not fit into the categories that follow, but they may serve as a starting point for beginning your own collection of images.

My photographs of water images were the inspiration for a quilt. Photo: Keith Tidball

Organization by Theme

Choosing a particular theme is an easy way to begin collecting images that interest you. It is amazing how simply concentrating on a theme heightens your senses. For example, I began to collect images of stairs, steps, and spiral staircases. Once I started with this theme, I began to see all types of staircases I had not noticed before in my everyday surroundings. My collection inspired *Spirals I*. Later, I began to notice stripes in the places where I had only seen staircases.

To get yourself started, choose a theme from the following list and collect as many images as you can find.

Stripes	Reflections	Textures	Baskets	Buttons
Brickwork	Bridges	Rivers	Water	Maps
Shoes	Trees	Gardens	Ponds	Fish
Insects	Tiles	Plastic objects	Pebbles	Stones
Beaches	Shells	Skeletons	Candies	Cakes
Food	Teapots	Trees	Pattern	Architectural detail

Emotional Connections

Important events in your life will affect your work, whether you intend them to or not. To explore emotional connections, you may choose to collect images that are connected in some way to personal memories, experiences, dreams, or stories that are meaningful to you. The images you collect will help you develop ideas into a visual language.

Political Beliefs

Many quilters use their art to express powerful feelings on such issues as war, peace, religion, conservation, or human suffering. A quilt can be your way of communicating opinions on something you believe in. Collecting images related to the issue that interests you will provide interesting starting points for your work.

Inspiration from Other Artists

The work of other artists—not just quiltmakers but artists from all media—is one of the richest sources of inspiration and can teach you a great deal about your own work. I attend as many exhibitions in as broad a range of media as I can, including textiles, painting, sculpture, and various crafts. If you like the subject matter another artist has chosen, rather than taking images directly from that artist's work, think of collecting similar images to work with yourself. Though the source of inspiration may be the same, the work you create will be entirely your own. Shows that feature a single artist, showing how his or her work has developed over the years, can be very motivating. Try not, however, to be in awe of another artist's work, no matter how much you admire it. It is far more productive to ask yourself questions that will help you understand your own development as an artist. Why do I like this work? What made the artist choose and develop this image? Why did the artist choose these colors? You may not be able to answer questions like these, but thinking them through will bring you much more in tune with your own likes and dislikes, helping you develop your own visual language.

Developing your understanding of the two topics covered in this Workshop—color and image—is at the very heart of any original work. Many of the quilters I meet in the Workshops I conduct feel that they do not handle color well. This is a stumbling block that deters them from even beginning a new quilt. The main thing I try to do is to persuade them to spend time thinking about color, and projects like the ones in this Workshop are very effective at making them do just that. Simply by putting time into thinking about color and about your color preferences, you gradually become fluent with its use. The same goes for collecting images—the more images you collect around a theme that is meaningful to you, the more confident you will be in creating a quilt that reflects that theme.

Studio Quilts

Paxton Study I (detail). Full quilt shown on page 48. Photo: Keith Tidball

Both *Joining Forces* (see page 19) and *Paxton Study I* were devised from observing colors and images from nature. The red and blue colors of "Coral Trout" (see page 107) and the shape, form, and color observation of the water reflections were the attractions in that work. In my excitement, I rather exaggerated the color. *Angela's Garden III* is one of my color study series, in which I observed and worked directly with colors from the natural world. Color alone can be full of energy and emotion. It is powerful stuff to work with!

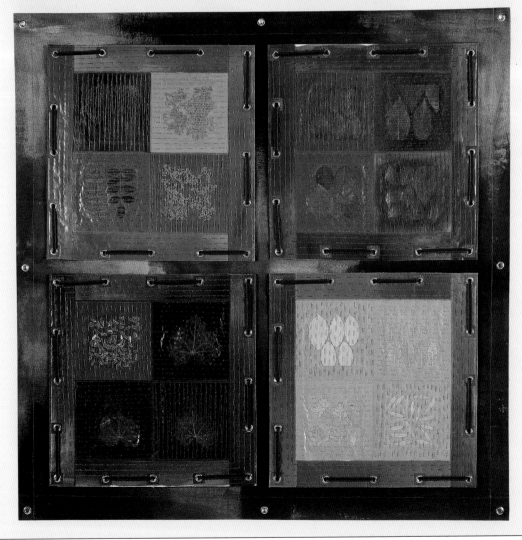

Angela's Garden III, 1997, 38" × 38" (97 cm × 97 cm). Photo: Keith Tidball

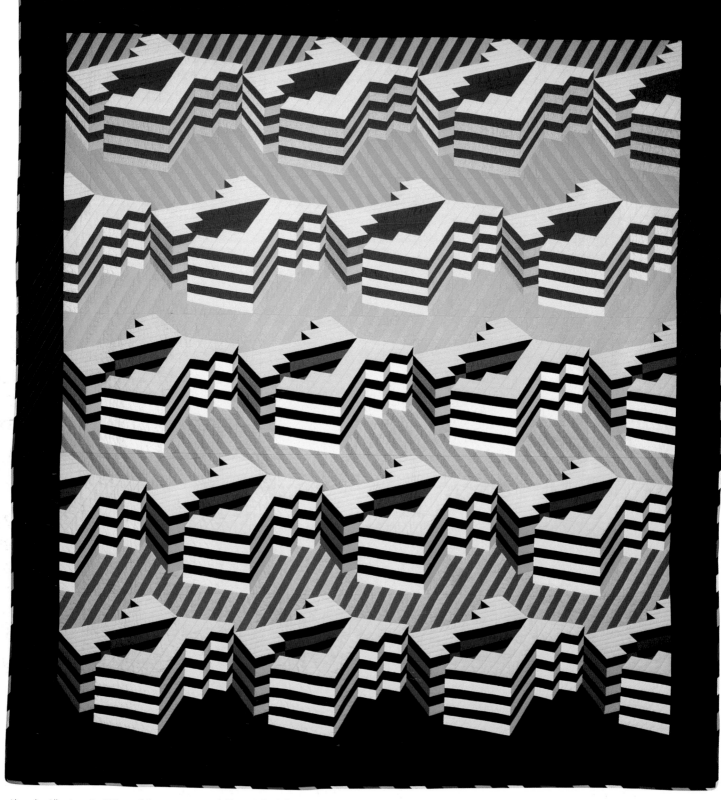

Liquorice Allsorts, 1983, 88" × 95" (223 cm × 241 cm). Photo: John Coles, Cornwall

Geometric 3-D Design Workshop | CHAPTER 7

In this Workshop, we will create original three-dimensional shapes for patchwork. These are flat, geometric patterns that have an illusion of depth. I have used this distinctive technique in several of my quilts, including *Eternal Triangle* (see page 77), *Cubic Pyramid* (see page 54), and *Mirrored Steps* (see page 85). The Workshop builds upon the piecing skills and the color sensibility you developed in earlier chapters. Piecing is the technique best suited to assembling the straight, crisp, hard-edged geometric forms characteristic of my 3-D designs. To create the illusion of depth, you must first be able to manipulate color and tone.

Most of the projects in this Workshop center around the cube shape, which most quilters will associate with the traditional quilt pattern *Tumbling Blocks*. Using the cube as a starting point, we will develop several designs, including one in which we work within the cube, altering its proportions. Other more complex design projects follow, using isometric and other graph papers to produce original 3-D shapes.

Liquorice Allsorts (detail). Photo: John Coles, Cornwall

WORKSHOP SUPPLIES

- General drawing equipment
- General sewing equipment, including sewing machine
- Paper and fabric scissors
- Ruler

- Graph paper, both square grid and isometric grid
- Circular graph paper (use a ruler, thumbtack, and string to make)
- Plain drawing paper, tracing paper

- Thin cardboard, glue, string, and drawing pin
- Colored pencils or crayons
- ¼-yd (0.25-m) strips—three dark tones, three medium tones, three light tones (check that they work well as a group)

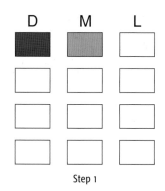

Step 1

Since the pressure with which you push on the pencil or crayon can change the tonal value of a color, try to pick out an entirely different color for each rectangle. This is hard, but it does get you thinking about tone.

Project 23 | **Using Tone for 3-D Effects**

It is use of color that gives depth to 3-D designs. This simple exercise will refresh the understanding of color and tone that you developed in Chapter 6. It will get you thinking about color before you start working with geometric shapes.

1. On a piece of plain drawing paper, draw a series of rectangles, measuring about 1" × 1½" (2.5 cm × 4 cm). Place them in three columns, labeled dark, medium, and light. Using dark, medium, and light gray or white pencils or crayons, color in the top row.
2. Spread out a full range of colored pencils or crayons and select one at random. Try out the color on a scrap of paper, then decide which column it belongs in. Color in the appropriate rectangle. Repeat with new random colors until the page is full.
3. Hold the paper out in front of you and study the tones. (It can help to squint—this separates the tones a little.) Compare tones across each column. Note that a color that seems dark in one row may be medium in another. Compare your rectangles across the page and occasionally glance at the top row to reference the dark, medium, and light tones.

Project 24 | **Cube Designs**

In this project we take a standard cube shape and design within it. The tonal exercise in the previous project now comes into play. Using color and tone carefully will help emphasize the cube shape. Many, many designs can spring from this project. Once the project is complete, we will make a cube unit in fabric. Before you begin, you will need to sketch out a cube shape on paper and decide how you will divide it for piecing. The simplest way to machine-piece a cube is to divide the top diamond into two triangles, as shown. The cube is now made up of two diamonds and two triangles. It is easy to work in a sequential order, through each column.

An alternative approach is to divide your cube up into six triangles. Keep in mind that with this layout, it is easy to lose the three-dimensional effect of the pattern. You will need to pay special attention to tone. Pair the triangles together and color them in dark, medium, and light tones to re-create the cube.

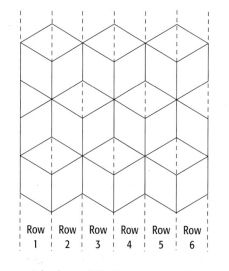

Row 1 | Row 2 | Row 3 | Row 4 | Row 5 | Row 6

Cube shapes divided for machine piecing

Cube layout design

To transfer tracing-paper designs, simply turn the tracing paper over and mark the lines of the design again on the reverse side. Then, place the tracing paper right-side-up over the next triangle and trace by lightly penciling over the original design lines. The tracing paper acts as a carbon, helping you re-create the exact design quickly and easily.

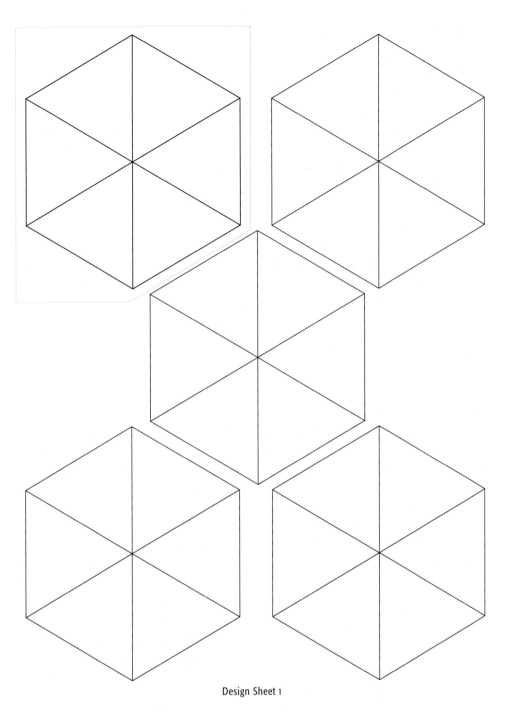

Design Sheet 1

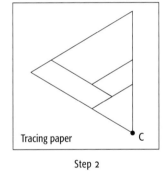

Tracing paper   • C

Step 2

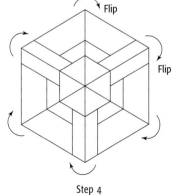

Flip

Flip

Step 4

1. Use Design Sheet 1. Within one of the triangles on the first cube, draw two or three straight lines. They can either go from edge to edge of the triangle or they can butt up against other drawn lines.

2. Trace the triangle, marking in pencil both its outline and the ruled lines within it. Mark the central point of the triangle with a C.

3. Flip the tracing paper over and trace a mirror image of the lines onto the next triangle in the same cube on the design sheet.

4. Repeat Step 2 until all the lines are drawn into each triangle in the cube, creating a symmetrical pattern.

Try using blacks, grays, and whites only on one of your design sheets. Establish where the tone is going to be placed. Then, on a second design sheet, replace the blacks, grays, and whites with color, sorted into tonal values.

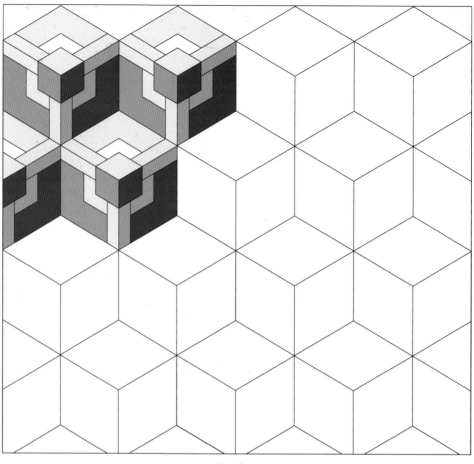

Design Sheet 2

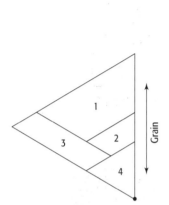

Step 9

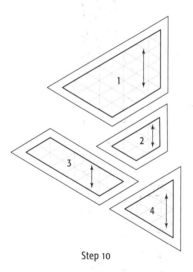

Step 10

Generally, it is best to keep the grain of the fabric running from top to bottom of a quilt. The cube shape is one exception. Here, keep the grain constant in each triangle, following one edge.

5. Shade the design, taking care with tone to make sure you achieve the illusion of depth.

6. Using Design Sheet 2, redraw several cubes with your pattern. (Design Sheet 2 is scaled down so that you can see the repeats.) Choose three or four colored pencils or crayons each in dark, medium, and light tones. Color the cubes on your design sheet, using tone to achieve a three-dimensional effect and to re-establish the cube shape.

7. Using the same technique, try out several alternate designs.

8. Choose the design you like best to make in fabric. To begin, enlarge one triangle of the original design to the size you require it to be in fabric. Draw it onto isometric graph paper. To help determine the final size, look at the smallest shape and visualize it in fabric. Make it large enough so that it will handle easily when cutting and sewing. (See section on scaling up on pages 60–61.)

9. Trace the drawing and number the shapes identically on the original and on the tracing. Take care with the numbering–this will be your sewing order.

10. Cut up the graph-paper drawing into the individual shapes and paste them onto cardboard to make templates. Mark the grain on the templates (as shown in the drawing to the left).

11. Refer back to your colored design and cut out the shapes from fabric.

12. Piece each triangle together. Keep the triangles separate until you decide the whole layout of your quilt. Then sew them together, row by row, including any border shapes you may require.

Here are two more complex designs made using the techniques in Project 24.

The first design, *Eternal Triangle*, is made up from just three templates—two triangles in different sizes and a diamond. The second, *Cubic Log Cabin*, is set onto a diamond, making it difficult to piece. The whole diamond block shape has to be set in—not an easy sewing task (see page 8, Method 1).

Eternal Triangle, 1983, 66" × 66" (167 cm × 167 cm). Photo: John Coles, Cornwall

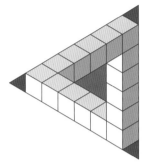

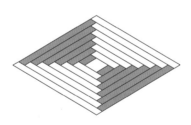

Cubic Log Cabin, 1982, 71" × 66" (180 cm × 167 cm). Photo: John Coles, Cornwall

DESIGNING WITH GRAPH PAPER

Sketching out patterns on graph paper, as we did in the preceding projects, is an easy way to begin a new design, either for single blocks or for a full quilt. It is a particularly useful technique when you are trying to achieve three-dimensional effects, since you can develop and color the entire design before you even begin to cut fabric. Working on top of a grid helps you keep drawings in balance, maintain symmetry, and create simple or complex designs with easy-to-piece geometric shapes. It also helps you work out color schemes that will create the illusion of depth.

Isometric graph paper is a wonderfully simple tool to help you create pattern upon pattern with geometric shapes. The paper itself can inspire the shapes you make, and every design unit created from this background grid will interlock perfectly, making the resulting quilt block easy to piece.

To experiment with isometric graph paper, collect a few images for inspiration. Look at photographs or magazine images of steps, stairs, boxes, tiles, or architectural details. Choose shapes you like and draw them onto isometric paper. Color them in dark, medium, and light tones to create an immediate three-dimensional effect. The

Pyramid II, 1980, 36″ × 32″ (92 cm × 81 cm). Photo: Pauline Burbidge

designs here were all drawn onto squared or isometric graph paper. Notice how the images change depending on how you color them. Notice, too, that they are all very easy to piece. (See also *Pyramid II* on page 78 and *The Final Pyramid* on page 7.)

It is also possible to find other graph papers, such as perspective charts, hypometric graph paper, or continuous sectional rolls. Just keep a lookout for different types and experiment with them. Using the charted lines as a guide, all sorts of unusual designs are possible.

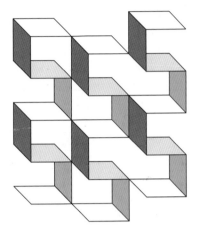

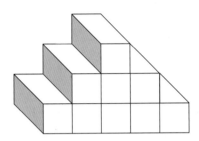

Three-dimensional designs on square graph paper

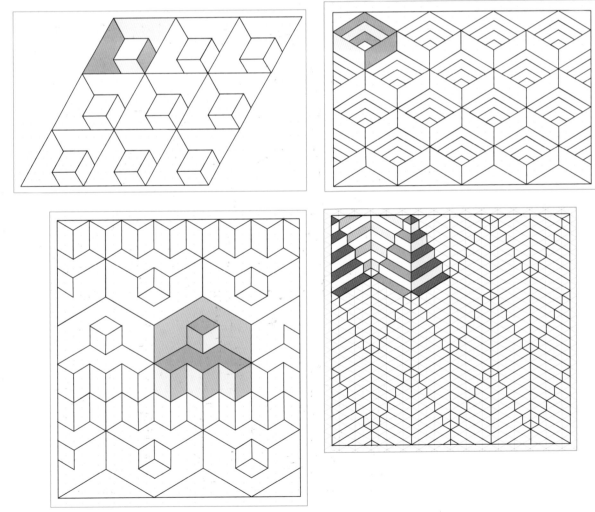

Three-dimensional designs on isometric graph paper

Circular Series, No. 3, 1984, 38" × 38" (97 cm × 97 cm).
Photo: John Coles, Cornwall

Circular Series No. 7, 1984, 36" × 36" (92 cm × 92 cm).
Photo: John Coles, Cornwall

DESIGNING WITH CIRCULAR GRAPH PAPER

Amazing designs can be mapped out using circular graph paper as a guide. Circular graph paper is available through specialty sources, but it is easy to make—all you will need is a ruler, a thumbtack, and a piece of string.

Work on a surface into which you can push a thumbtack. Use the thumbtack to hold a piece of string in place at one corner of a large square of plain drawing paper (the size of your finished block or quilt). Tie a pencil to the other end of the string at a measured distance from the tack. Use the pencil as a compass to draw a curved line across the paper. Draw additional parallel curved lines at regular intervals. Use a ruler and pencil to draw the straight lines that fan out from the corner. Map in your design, using the technique described in Project 24, and make your templates. (For small designs, a compass may be easier to use.)

The two photos at the top of the page are two unusual designs I created using circular graph paper. Each is based on a quarter circle. It is easy to repeat the design three more times to end up with a complete circular quilt design.

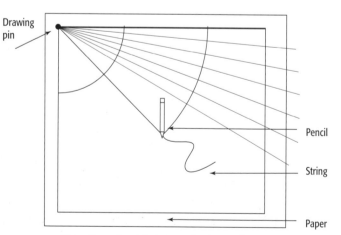

Three-dimensional designs on circular graph paper

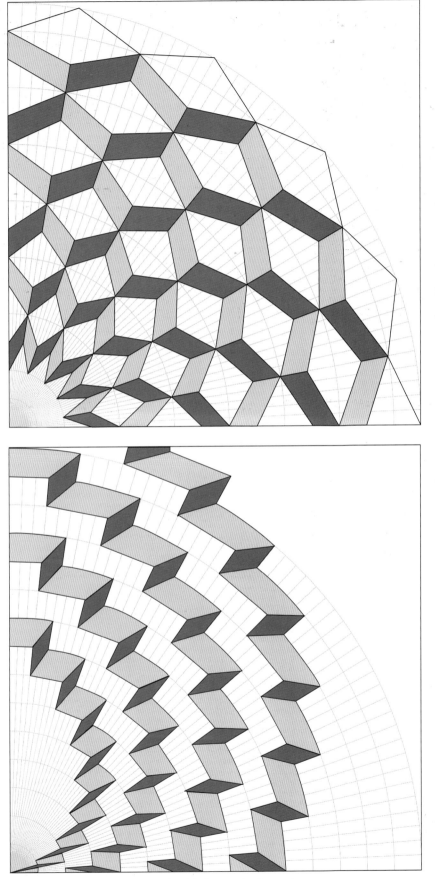

Three-dimensional designs on circular graph paper

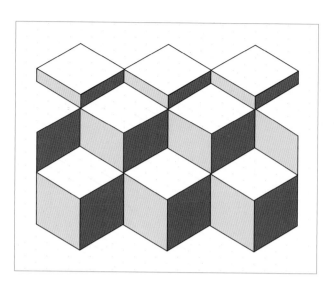

Design A: here, the height of the cube is constant, but the width shrinks as the design moves from right to left.

Design B: here, the width of the cube is constant, but the height changes.

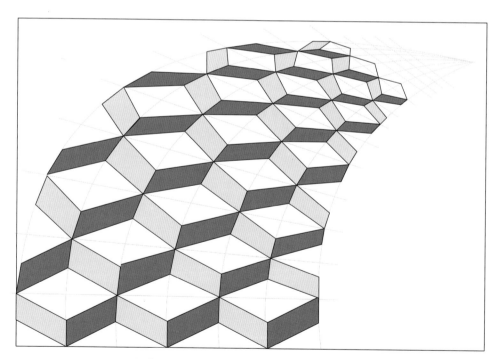

Design C: distorting an image by drawing a new grid

DISTORTING THE IMAGE

There is no need to feel bound to strictly geometric designs when working with grids. It is possible to vary the design in any way you choose simply by distorting the shape once you have laid it out onto graph paper. For example, you can distort the width of the cube while keeping the height constant (Design A). Conversely, you can squash the height of the cube but keep the width constant (Design B).

Another approach is to draw your own graph construction lines, creating a new grid in which to plan your design. In Design C I drew in the construction lines with a pliable curving ruler, then mapped in the cubed shapes. In a design like this, each shape is different and therefore requires its own template.

There is an incredible amount of potential in the projects included in this Workshop. Once you understand how the designs are put together from simple geometrics, you can develop a style that is all your own. Try sketching some three-dimensional objects that appeal to you. Your sketches may suggest other ideas. You can repeat the projects in this chapter over and over again, as each time the results will be entirely different.

Studio Quilts

The designs we created in this Workshop all developed from graph-paper shapes. As we saw, *Cubic Log Cabin* (see page 77) and *Eternal Triangle* (see page 77) were both created using the cube design technique described in Project 24. *Cubic Pyramid* (see page 54) was designed with isometric graph paper. I used circular graph paper for all the quilts in the series *Circular Quilts*. It is also possible to achieve a three-dimensional design by working with actual three-dimensional objects. In the quilts *Mirrored Steps* (page 85), *Liquorice Allsorts* (page 72), and *Spirals I* (page 85), I worked from still-life models. I placed the models in front of two mirrors, set at a 60° angle. The reflected shapes were kaleidoscopic in nature, forming intricate patterns. I studied these images, drew them, and photographed them. They were the source of several finished designs for a series of quilts.

Cubic Pyramid (detail). See full quilt on page 54.
Photo: John Coles, Cornwall

Chequered Cube, 1982, 108″ × 48″
(274 cm × 122 cm)

Mirrored Steps, 1983, 79" × 83" (200 cm × 210 cm). Photo: John Coles, Cornwall

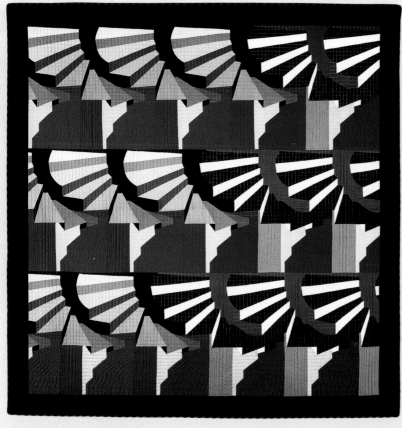

Spirals I, 1985, 90" × 88" (228 cm × 223 cm). Photo: John Coles, Cornwall

Design for *Spirals I*, 1985

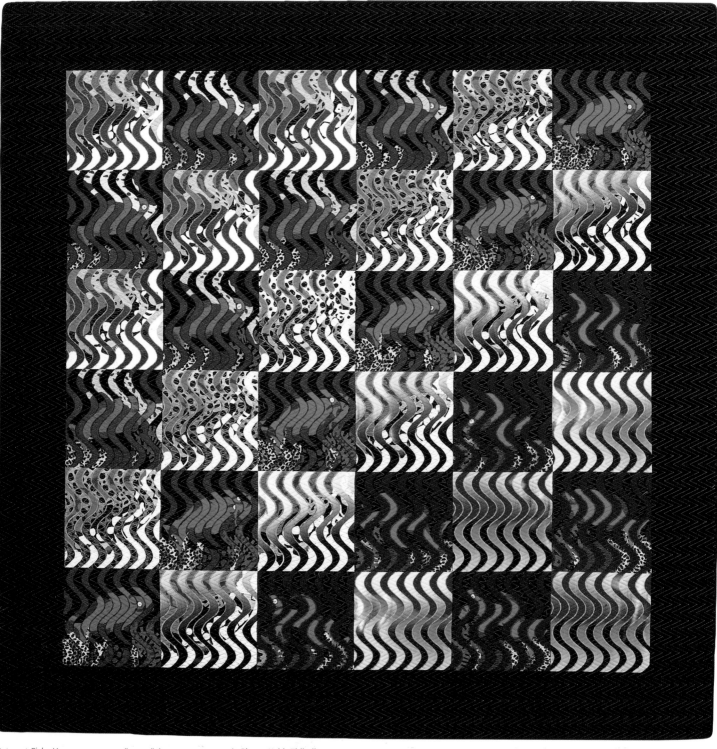

Intercut Fish–Harmony, 1991, 79" × 79" (200 cm × 200 cm). Photo: Keith Tidball

Pattern and Repeated Block Workshop

CHAPTER 8

The definition of the word *pattern* that I like best is "a regularly repeating arrangement of lines, shapes, or colors on a surface, that has or is intended to have a decorative or pleasing effect" (*The Longman Dictionary of Contemporary English*). Pattern is found all around us, both in nature and in art. As quilters, we can draw inspiration not only from traditional block designs but from architectural detail, from brickwork, tiles, and slates, and from plant life and shell forms, to name but a few.

Quiltmaking has a long and rich tradition of block patterns. Each block has a name and, like tile patterns, once blocks repeat, larger patterns emerge as if by magic. This is one of the characteristics of quiltmaking that first attracted me. There is an appeal to ordered, repeated images and an indescribable delight in discovering intricate patterns within them.

Intercut Fish–Harmony (detail). Photo: Keith Tidball

WORKSHOP SUPPLIES

- General drawing equipment, including a selection of black marker pens, pencils, and colored crayons
- General sewing equipment, including sewing machine and sewing threads
- Paper and fabric scissors

- Graph paper, both square grid and iso-metric grid
- Plain white drawing paper, black paper, tracing paper
- Cutting board and cutting blade or scalpel
- Glue stick, masking tape

- Soft paintbrush (medium) and tube of black gouache paint, a water-based opaque paint that gives a flat, solid surface
- Collection of still-life objects—favorite fabrics, bowls, vases, dishes, boxes, etc.
- Selection of colored solid (or plain) fabrics, including black and white

Traditional block patterns

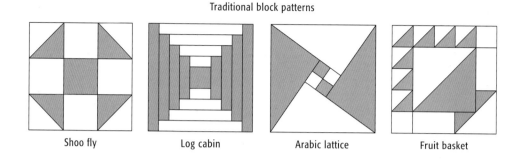

Shoo fly   Log cabin   Arabic lattice   Fruit basket

The aim of this Workshop is to explore some of the many ways of creating repeating patterns, as well as offering a few notes on design experiments with pattern. Most of the projects are in black and white, so that you can focus clearly on the shape and form of patterns. The first projects are simple and progress toward more complex designs. By the end of the Workshop, you will be able to develop individual themes using common techniques. This is an essential Workshop for quiltmakers, but will also be of great interest to you if you are involved in other surface design media.

| Project 25 | **Repeating Squares** |

Most traditional quilt blocks are based on a simple square unit, the most versatile of all geometric shapes. This simple exercise can be done again and again for an amazing number of different effects.

1. Draw six 2″ (5 cm) squares on a sheet of white paper. Butt them together in the center of the paper, leaving some space around the outside edges. Use a ruler to help you draw one line anywhere within the first square.

2. Copy the same line in the identical position in the other five squares.

3. Take one more sheet of white paper and two of black in the same size. Stack them with the black sheets on the bottom and the drawing on top, as shown. Tape them down onto a cutting board.

Step 3

4. Using a scalpel, slice through all layers, first cutting along the lines drawn inside the squares, and second, the actual outer edges of the squares. You will have several identical shapes in both black and white.

5. Using these cut out shapes arrange two nine-patch block designs, showing different patterns. To experiment with different layouts, look at page 89. If you like one of the designs, you may want to cut up more identical shapes to create a larger study than the nine-patch block.

6. Repeat Steps 1 to 5, using a curved line rather than a straight line.

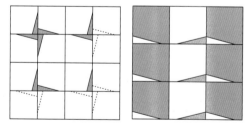

Step 5

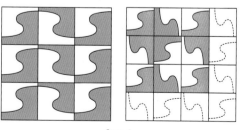

Step 6

Repeating Simple Blocks

Most of the projects in this chapter are based on simple square and triangular units. There are several ways in which you can repeat these shapes across a quilt for a variety of effects. In this Workshop, we will refer to six classic ways of repeating blocks: standard repeat, rotating repeat, mirror repeat, half-slide repeat, half-drop repeat, and checkerboard repeat. Checkerboard repeat can be applied to any of the layout designs.

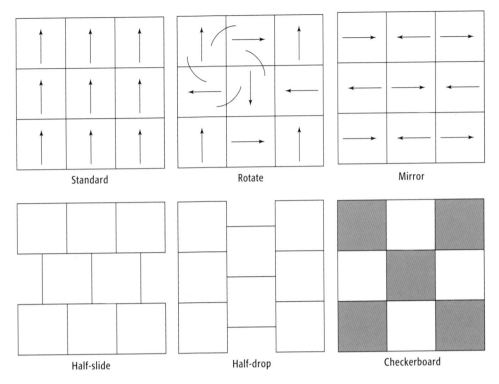

Standard   Rotate   Mirror

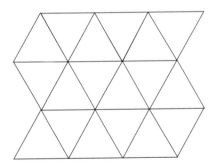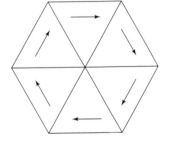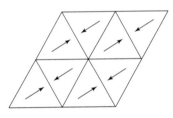

Half-slide   Half-drop   Checkerboard

Six techniques for repeating patterns with a square unit

Standard   Rotate   Mirror

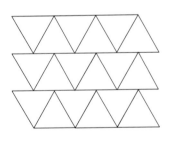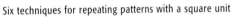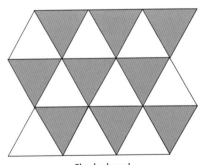

Half-slide   Half-drop   Checkerboard

Six techniques for repeating patterns with a triangular unit

Repeating Tessellated Shapes

The squares you worked with in the previous project are simple *tessellations*—shapes that will interlock perfectly to repeat across a surface. There are no overlaps or gaps between the units when tessellated shapes are put together—they fit perfectly on all sides. This characteristic makes them ideal as patchwork shapes. Squares and rectangles both tessellate, as shown. On square graph paper, simply arrange them in patterns without gaps or overlaps. Shade in black and white to accentuate patterns. You can create your own tessellating shapes from a square or rectangle quite easily. Simply slice a piece out of the original shape and move it to another side, as shown. Rearrange multiples of this new pattern to create a tessellating design. The designs shown in Design 2 at right are created by simply repeating rectangles: A is a half-slide pattern; in B some shapes are placed horizontally and others vertically; and in C the rectangles are rotated. This last design comes slightly outside the boundaries of a true tessellation, as it creates an extra shape—a square—that has to be placed between the rectangles. Design 3 is an example of slicing a section off the rectangle to create a new interlocking shape. The shapes in Designs 4, 5, and 6 are drawn using square graph paper. Designs 5 and 6 fit neatly into square units, whereas Design 4 is a shape that interlocks perfectly with itself.

Using isometric paper, you can also create tessellations from triangles or parallelograms. In Design 7 identical shapes are made by drawing around the isometric graph lines, as with Design 8. This is an interlocking triangle, and A, B, and C illustrate the different layouts that can be assembled. Design 9, the parallelogram, can be drawn on isometric paper. It can be treated as a basic unit that could house more pattern within it. (See *Stripey Step 1* on page 99.)

Design 1:
Square

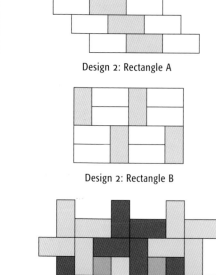

Design 2: Rectangle A

Design 2: Rectangle B

Design 2: Rectangle C

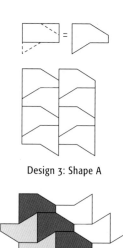

Design 3: Shape A

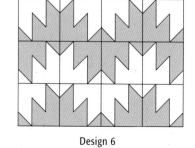

Design 3: Shape B

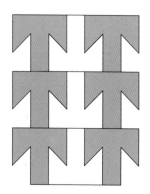

Design 4

Design 5

Design 6

Design 7

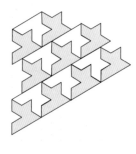

Design 8: Pattern A

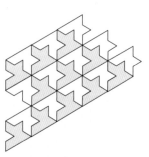

Design 8: Pattern B

Design 8: Pattern C

Design 9

Experimenting with Repeating Patterns

There is no better way to find out which images work best in repeat patterns than to try them out. However, there are certain qualities to look out for. The first two images at right do not work well. Avoid floating an image completely in the center of a block—this will not repeat well. Avoid, too, having evenly sized shapes over the entire image area—you will lose any sense of a repeating pattern. The next two ideas *do* work well. Have the balance of the images slightly lopsided or asymmetrical. Also, vary the design with shapes that are of different scales. Try balancing points at the same measurement along the sides of the block, so that you can link them when the pattern repeats.

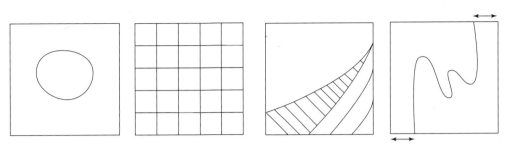

These two do not work well.   These two work better.

Photomontage

As an alternative, instead of working directly from a still-life setup, use your camera to create images. Take photographs of details, focusing at close range. Choose the best image and develop eight prints. Arrange them into a repeat pattern. If you require a mirror image print for your layout design, take a print from the reverse side of a transparency.

Photomontage, 1993. Photo:
Pauline Burbidge

Pattern in Nature

The repeated forms in nature show us wonderful harmony. There are many forms that show repeating shapes—but with a difference. Every leaf, every shell, every wave in the ocean is similar but never identical. This organic, flowing quality is far more exciting to me than exact repeats of identical shapes. This image of an Australian palm trunk is an example. Each overlapping leaf has a similar structure, but no two are identical. The formation of the plant reminds me of the *Log Cabin* quilt block, but without that characteristic rigid regularity of the traditional block layout.

Palm Trunk, Australia, 1988. Photo:
Pauline Burbidge

Project 26 | **Repeating a Still-Life Block**

Still-life setups created from a selection of favorite objects are a unique and rich source of repeating block patterns. The beauty is that you can repeat this exercise over and over again, producing completely different patterns every time.

1. Set up your still-life objects, and, as in Project 29 in Chapter 9, select an area of the still life from which to work. Cut a small window measuring about 1" (2.5 cm) square in a piece of cardboard, and use this to view your still life and select an image. As an example, look at my paper collage, "Intercut Block 2," on page 94.
2. Make a simple line drawing, about 2" (5 cm) square, of the selected image area.
3. Trace the block and, referring back to the six classic ways of repeating blocks on page 89, work out some alternative repeating patterns. Draw the layout you like best in pencil.
4. Make several photocopies and try out different color ideas on each. Begin with black, gray, and white so that you have a clear idea of the effect of tones.

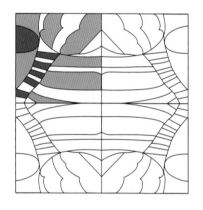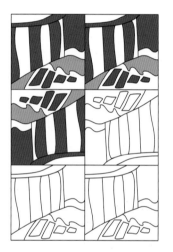

Layouts from a still life

Project 27 | **Line Repeat**

This project is very effective for designing border patterns or for designing patterned strips that run across a quilt.

1. Draw a horizontal line across a sheet of graph paper about 2" to 3" (5 cm to 7.5 cm) from the top edge. Draw a shape above the line. The shape must start and finish on the line and must be at its widest along the line, too, as shown. Trace the shape, including the horizontal line.

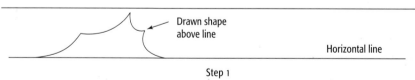

Drawn shape
above line

Horizontal line

Step 1

2. Turn the tracing over and draw over all lines in soft pencil.
3. Turn the tracing back to the right side and swivel so that the shape is now below the horizontal line. Link it to the end of the first shape drawn, and trace.
4. Continue, drawing one shape above and one shape below the horizontal line, until you have covered the width of the page. Experiment with additional designs.

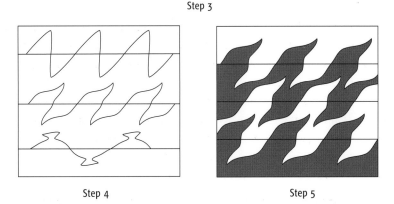

Step 3

Step 4

Step 5

5. Choose one of your designs and draw three rows onto a new sheet of paper. Using gouache paint, fill in the design in black and white. Repeat with a new set of rows, this time filling in an alternate pattern. Notice how drastically the design can change according to how you position and space the rows.

Project 28 | **Continuous Line Drawing with Pattern**

Sometimes, working with geometric repeated blocks can seem rigid. This project loosens up hard-edged designs, giving them a little more flow. This technique of creating more free-form patterns is particularly appealing when trying to re-create the repeating patterns found in nature. It is a way of giving hard-edged geometric forms more organic life!

1. Choose one of the straight-line layouts you produced in Project 25. Pin your design to the wall where you can see it easily from your drawing table. Study it carefully, planning how you will be able to redraw it.

2. Using a drawing board and drawing paper or a sketch pad, pencil in the design. Try to draw in continuous lines, never lifting the pencil from the paper. Keep your eyes glued to the design on the wall, not on the sketch you are making.

3. Repeat until you are satisfied with the free, fluid lines of the redrawn design.

4. To avoid the straight-line, precise effect that piecing creates, make up your design in appliqué or fabric collage. By doing so, you will be able to re-create the soft, flowing lines of the design in fabric.

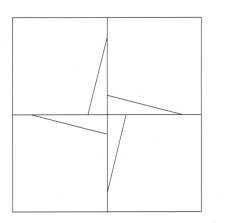

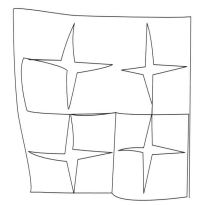

Step 2

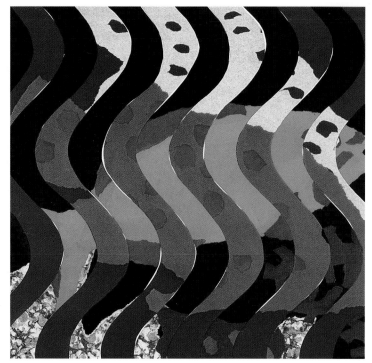

"Intercut Block 1" (paper collage), 1991,
12" × 12" (30 cm × 30 cm). Photo:
Keith Tidball

"Intercut Block 2" (paper collage), 1991,
12" × 12" (30 cm × 30 cm). Photo:
Keith Tidball

Here are some examples of how you might decide to cut your blocks. Place your tracing paper design over your blocks to make sure you like the result.

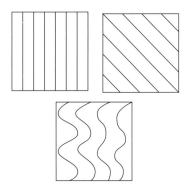

Examples of how to cut blocks

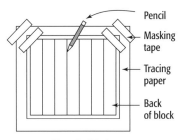

Marking the block

OTHER EXPERIMENTS IN DESIGNING PATTERN

Intercutting Blocks

I have made several quilts using the technique of *intercutting*. It involves making up two blocks in the same size but with different images. The blocks are then cut up in exactly the same way and the images are intermixed. *Intercut Fish—Harmony* on page 86 and *Joining Forces II* on page 107 are both examples. Before you mesh the images together, it is impossible to tell what the result will be. I enjoy the random nature of the technique—sometimes I'm disappointed by the finished block, but other times I am thrilled.

Here is an example of how I made the intercut blocks in these quilts. This process could be applied to any designs. I am going to illustrate intercutting two blocks with completely different designs so that you can easily see what is going on. The blocks were exactly the same size. The first was an image of a fish; the second was made up of wavy lines, representing water.

Two collage blocks

I ironed fusible web (Bondaweb or Wonder-Under) onto the whole surface of the back of each block, leaving the backing paper in place. Next, I decided how to cut the blocks, settling on vertical lines, which I then drew onto tracing paper with a soft pencil.

I placed the tracing paper, pencil lines down, on top of the fusible web on the reverse of the first block. Taping both the tracing and the fabric block down to prevent them from moving, I ran a pencil over the back of the lines, so that the impression was left on the backing paper of the fusible web. I marked the second block in exactly the same way. Next, I cut both blocks along the marked lines.

I then cut two pieces of thin muslin, ½" (1.5 cm) larger than the blocks on all sides. I took alternating strips from each block and began to assemble two intercut images, peeling off the fusible web backing and positioning each strip in place. Once the whole block was assembled, I ironed everything in place. I used a wide zigzag stitch to stitch over the cut lines. To see the effect on a finished quilt, look at *Intercut Fish — Harmony* on page 86.

To avoid disappointments when practicing this technique, try intercutting with paper blocks rather than fabric. You can then make the intercut designs that work best in fabric and arrange them in repeats to complete a quilt top.

Changing the Scale of Blocks

You can achieve some very interesting and unusual effects using repeating blocks by varying the scale on the same quilt top. For example, if you scale square blocks down to quarter the original size, two of the smaller blocks will fit onto one side of the original block. This forms a good link and varies the pace of the quilt. As another example, you can arrange columns of larger images next to columns of more intense, smaller blocks. You could go one stage further and repeat this process, scaling the block down in size again to make it a quarter the size of the smaller block, as shown.

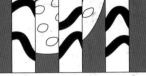

Intercut blocks

With the square blocks you can create an instant border pattern for a quilt, with the smaller blocks on the outside edge. You can also try this scaling-down process with triangular blocks and parallelograms. The technique, coupled with simple block designs, can make a very exciting project.

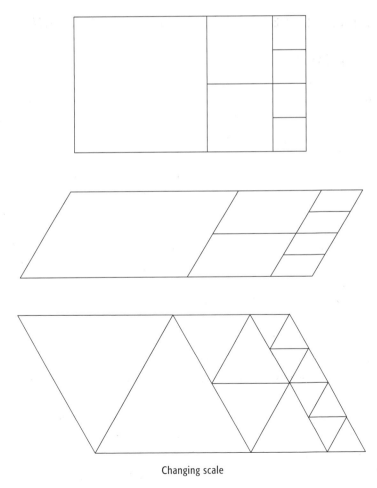

Changing scale

Building Up Images with Pattern

Here are a few more ideas you can use to design with pattern.

Rubbings

Rubbings on surfaces can be used to build up images. To make a rubbing, collect together various textured sheet materials, such as corrugated cardboard, plastic grid, embossed cardboard, wire mesh, wallpaper, etc. Draw a simple shape in outline on a sheet of thin paper. Placing the paper on top of each textured sample, scribble over sections of the design with a large wax crayon. In effect, you are taking a rubbing off each texture. Build your block design by scribbling in areas of pattern, using texture rather than line as a guide. You can make several different block designs using the same sheet materials and by varying pressure on the crayon and texturing areas of the outlined shape in different ways each time.

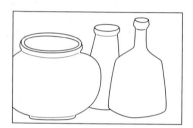

Still-life subject

Textured drawing of still life

Once you have completed drawings you like, there are many options open to interpret these in fabric. Textured areas could be made up of patterned fabrics, for example. Or textured fabrics could be created, using the same rubbing method and fabric crayons or fabric paints. You could also use fabric collage to re-create your textured drawings in fabric.

Flattening Shapes to Create Pattern

Aerial-view photographs of the landscape can be very inspirational. For example, mountaintops and meandering rivers viewed from above can become patterns for your quilts. A series of fields planted or plowed into strips forms wonderful two-dimensional patterns when viewed from the air.

On a smaller scale, too, viewing objects from above can inspire new patterns. Try, for example, a tabletop full of buttons, paper clips, or shells. Imagine the patterns made by a room full of ballroom dancers when viewed from above.

What makes pattern? A little lateral thinking on this topic might sow the seeds for some very original approaches for your quilts! I observe that pattern is made by placing or arranging shapes into an order, as these two photographs show. The first illustrates chaos—the tires are randomly piled up with no order; therefore no pattern. The second illustrates order—the tires are specifically arranged, creating pattern.

Tires, 1989. Photo: Pauline Burbidge

Tires, 1987. Photo: Pauline Burbidge

Observe patterns wherever you have the opportunity in the world around you. Collect images that appeal to you—magazine clippings, newspapers, wrappers, and photographs you take are all great sources. Pin them up in your work area and think about them as you work. Which patterns do you feel are the most successful and why? Which ones would transfer well into a quilt? The time you put into just thinking about patterns will help you develop a style of patterning that is truly your own.

Studio Quilts

The quilts shown here illustrate works all made with repeating blocks. *Heartbeat* and *Custard Squash II* were both designed from square blocks, using images taken from a still life. "Heartbeat Collage," for example, came from a detail of folded striped fabric. *Stripey Step I* uses geometric shapes that fit into a repeating parallelogram. *Striped Canopy* and *Lowestoft* are repeated rectangles containing detailed images of urban landscapes. *Striped Canopy* uses nine blocks, based on an image of a canopy draped over a fruit stall in a market square. A detail of a ship in dry dock was the subject for the block design of *Lowestoft*. I felt particularly happy with this finished design, as the repeat block tends to fuse with the whole surface of the quilt.

Heartbeat, 1993, 42" × 42" (107 cm × 107 cm). Photo: Keith Tidball

Heartbeat Collage, 1993, 12" × 12" (30 cm × 30 cm). Photo: Keith Tidball

Custard Squash II, 1989, 59" × 66" (150 cm × 167 cm). Photo: Keith Tidball

Stripey Step I, 1984, 71″ × 66″ (180 cm × 167 cm). Photo: John Coles, Cornwall

Lowestoft, 1987, 58″ × 55″ (147 cm × 140 cm). Photo: John Coles, Cornwall

Striped Canopy, 1990, 121″ × 96″ (307 cm × 244 cm). Photo: Keith Tidball

The Pink Fish, 1991, 84″ × 84″ (213 cm × 213 cm). Photo: Keith Tidball

Paper Collage and Fabric Collage Workshop

CHAPTER 9

Paper collage is a great way to begin designing for fabric collage. Both have similar qualities; both use solid areas of color, rather than line, to create an image. To create a paper collage image, all you need do is simply tear or cut pieces of paper and glue them onto a backing paper. Fabric collage is built up by laying fabric shapes, backed with fusible web such as Bondaweb or Wonder-Under, onto a base cloth. You then iron them in place and stitch over them to secure them. Fabric collage is an interesting nontraditional quiltmaking technique that has developed from appliqué methods.

In this Workshop we will first produce two paper collage studies from a still life. From these, we will then select an image from which to design a block in fabric. Four blocks will be made up. You may use these as the starting point for any quiltmaking project, large or small.

The Pink Fish (detail). Photo: Keith Tidball

WORKSHOP SUPPLIES

- General drawing equipment
- General sewing equipment, including sewing machine and a selection of threads
- Paper and fabric scissors
- Tracing paper
- A few 12" (30 cm) sheets of medium to heavyweight drawing paper, white

- Wallpaper paste
- Two drawing boards, approximately 15" (40 cm) square
- Two household paintbrushes, approximately 1" (2.5 cm) wide
- Brown paper tape, approximately 2" (5 cm) wide
- Selection of objects for a still-life setup

- Selection of colored papers, at least letter size
- Selection of 100-percent-cotton fabrics in solid colors, including white for base
- Fusible web, such as Bondaweb or Wonder-Under

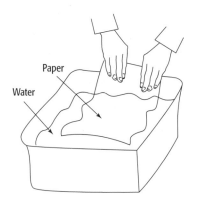

Paper

Water

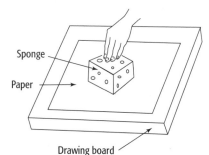

Sponge

Paper

Drawing board

Brown tape

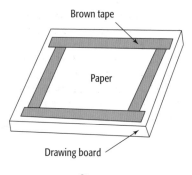

Paper

Drawing board

Step 1

Project 29 | **Paper Collage**

I find that one of the easiest ways to design quilt blocks is to begin by working in paper, later transferring pleasing designs onto fabric. Paper is a good medium in which to produce experimental designs. You discover quickly which designs will work and which will not. Here, we will make two paper collage studies, both 10″ (25 cm) square. We will make one in black and white and the other in color.

1. In order to avoid the paper buckling when applying the collage, first stretch two sheets of white paper onto drawing boards. There are two ways to do this—try both to decide which you prefer.
   - Tear off four lengths of brown paper tape, a little longer than the edges of the paper. Holding two corners of the paper, immerse it fully in a large container of water for a few seconds. Place it quickly, as squarely as you can, onto the drawing board. Use a sponge to absorb excess water, wiping it rapidly over the surface. Tape down with brown tape around all edges. Allow to dry flat, overnight if possible. The paper will wrinkle at first, but will then dry flat.
   - Place the dry paper on the drawing board. Dampen it thoroughly with a very wet sponge. Work rapidly for a few seconds only. When the paper is soaked, tape it down with brown tape around all edges. Allow to dry flat.

Still-life setup. Photo: Pauline Burbidge

2. Set up a still life, using objects that reflect your preferences in shape and color. Consider using objects that have a theme. For example, you may have a collection of striped or spotted objects that you wish to use. As well as taking care in choosing the objects, position them carefully. Think about the background and the spaces between the objects. Draped fabric or colored paper both make good background bases.
3. Select a portion of the still-life image. To do this, cut a small square window into a piece of white paper and move it around the image so that you can view the still life section by section. Try cutting two different window sizes—such as 1½″ (4 cm) square or 3″ (8 cm) square—to see how different the selected images become. Hold the window at arm's length and pass it over the still life until you find a portion that pleases you.
4. Make rough sketches of pleasing images to help you make a final selection. Remember to keep the sketches simple.

5. Mix a jar of wallpaper paste, slightly thicker than recommended by the manufacturer, and allow it to stand for 15 minutes.

6. Draw a 10" (25 cm) square onto each of your two pieces of stretched paper.

7. To begin the black and white collage, first study the tones in the selected portion of your still-life image, separating them into blacks, grays, and whites. (This is an excellent exercise to help you analyze the tones of colors and also to simplify images.)

8. Pick out the larger shapes and paste them down, filling the entire block. Then observe more detail, and work the collage to completion.

9. Repeat this process to complete the color collage. Select your range of colors before you begin, and again think of pasting down the largest areas first. Then, as before, work toward more detail. When you are near completion, view the collage from a distance and as often as you can. This will help you judge when the collage is complete. Remember that clear, bold shapes make the best collage—avoid too much fussy detail. As examples, look at the finished collages at the end of this chapter.

10. Pin your two paper studies up on the wall and choose one to work into a repeating block design.

11. Take a sheet of tracing paper and draw a 5" (12.5 cm) square on it. Pass this over the collage to select an area that will make a good repeating block. (See Chapter 8 for more on repeating blocks.) Trace the selected shapes.

To help form the shapes, mark the paper by folding it with one hand pressing the paper flat on the board and the other hand lifting it and folding it back to mark a crease. Either cut or tear this shape. A cut line creates a hard-edged shape, a torn edge a soft one. If you want a soft straight line, use a ruler to help tear the paper.

Folding and marking shapes

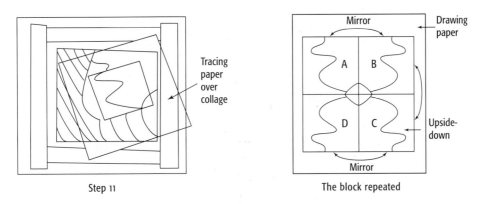

Step 11

The block repeated

To trace the design onto white paper, first turn the traced image upside down. With a soft pencil, draw over the lines that show through from the front, including the outer square. In effect, you are making a carbon copy. Place the tracing paper, reverse side down, on the white paper. With a harder pencil, draw over the original lines again. This will make an imprint, transferring the traced design onto the white paper beneath.

12. Onto a clean sheet of white paper, trace four blocks, laying them out as shown. Do not forget to draw the outer edges of the squares. Block A is identical to the image you traced in Step 11. Flip the tracing paper over into a mirror image to obtain Block B. From this position, flip the tracing again, forming a mirror image for Block C and then again for Block D. (Note that Blocks A and C are identical, as are blocks B and D.) Your design is now ready to transfer onto fabric.

Project 30 | **Transferring Paper Collage onto Fabric**

In this project, we will make just one block in fabric. It is always best to begin with a single block. Not only can you refine the design or color choices if necessary, but you can test your construction techniques. After making a single block, you will be able to work out quicker ways of making multiple blocks. Once you develop a rhythm, you will find that you can make as many as six blocks in the time it took you to make the first one!

1. Use the tracing paper drawing you made in the previous project as your "plan drawing." You will use this as a guide instead of templates. Mark the right side of the tracing paper and label areas of color (R = red, B = blue, Y = yellow).

How can you tell which part of the collage will make a good repeating block? Look again at page 91. Also, here are a few thoughts to consider:

• Avoid completely symmetrical designs with the shape floating in the middle.

• Try selecting shapes that have contrasting areas of different sizes.

• If your image has many right-angled shapes, try tilting it to create a more interesting repeat.

• Try choosing a shape that has a matching measurement on two sides of the block. This will allow you to interchange these matching sides when repeating.

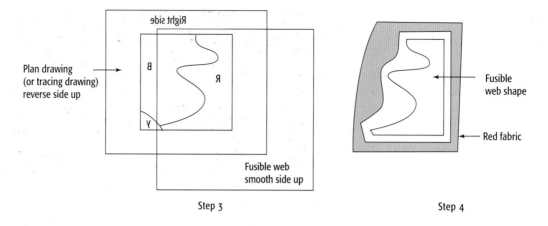

Step 3   Step 4

2. Cut out a base block from the white fabric measuring 6" (15 cm) square. This allows ½" (1.5 cm) seam allowances all around.

3. Turn the plan drawing over to show the reverse side. Place fusible web, such as Bondaweb or Wonder-Under, over it with the smooth paper side up. Trace one shape at a time onto the fusible web, beginning, in this example, with the red shape. If your design has several red shapes, collect them all together at this stage onto the fusible web.

4. Cut roughly around the shape, leaving at least ¼" (0.75 cm) extra around all edges. (This extra allowance prevents fraying once the fusible web is cut.) Iron the shape onto red fabric. When cool, cut around the shape on the drawn line.

5. Cut the blue and yellow shapes out in the same way.

6. Peel the backing paper off the shapes, leaving the dry fabric glue from the fusible web, and assemble the pieces glue-side down onto the white base block, remembering to position them ½" (1.5 cm) inside the outer edges of the block.

7. Double-check the correct positioning of the shapes by placing the plan drawing directly over the block. None of the fabric shapes are permanent until they are ironed. When you are satisfied with the placement, press the shapes onto the base block with a hot dry iron.

8. To match the layout sample you created in Step 11 of the previous project, make three more blocks in the same way. You will need one identical block (Block C) and two reverse-image blocks (Blocks B and D). Make these up.

9. In each block, stitch around the edges of the shapes using satin stitch or a stitch of your choice (see pages 17 and 18). Trim the completed blocks down to 5" (12.5 cm) square and turn them face down in the correct order, butting the edges together.

10. Cut 1" (2.5 cm) strips of fabric and iron fusible web onto the backs. Peel off the backing paper, place the strips over the joints between blocks, and iron.

11. On the right side, stitch the blocks together, either with a wide zigzag stitch or with free machine stitching. Quilt as desired.

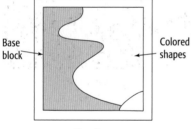

Base block ← → Colored shapes

Step 6

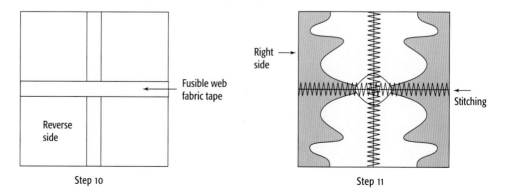

Step 10   Step 11

DEVELOPING FURTHER PROJECTS

Using paper and fabric collage, it is possible to produce an endless number of block designs that are inspired by images that surround you and that are unique to you. From a single design, you can create several different quilts, both by alternating colors and fabrics and by experimenting with block layouts. Chapter 8 provides more ideas for layout options.

The four blocks described in Project 30 are made into one unit. The stitching joins them together and forms an important part of the design. However, you may prefer to make these four blocks as a single unit. To do so, you would need to assemble them onto one whole piece of backing fabric. You would also cut out the central shapes as one shape, thus avoiding having a seam line run through the middle.

Another way to approach the project would be to use the entire paper collage image for the repeating block. Trace it and try a four-block repeat to see if it works well. Then simply trace your shapes off the paper collage and reproduce the study in fabric. You would end up with four 10" (25 cm) fabric blocks that combine into a 20" (50 cm) quilt.

Still Life I, 1986, 58" × 58" (147 cm × 147 cm). Photo: John Coles, Cornwall

You may be so pleased with your paper collage studies that you want to keep them. It's easy to frame them or use the same techniques to make one-of-a-kind greeting cards. You can develop your fabric collages in the same way, turning them into pillow covers, wall-hangings, or large-scale quilts. However you end up using them, creating paper and fabric collages is a wonderful way to explore color and shape. Your collages will also teach you a great deal about your personal color preferences.

Studio Quilts

I made my first major series of paper collages in 1986. I felt that "Still Life No. 10" was particularly successful. The collages "Sweetlips," "Coral Trout," and "Coffee Pot and Fish" all developed into major quilts, namely *Joining Forces* (see page 19), *Joining Forces II* (see opposite page), and *The Pink Fish* (see page 100). I hope you enjoy seeing the links between them and that they inspire you to experiment freely with both paper and fabric collage.

"Still Life No. 10" (paper collage), 1985, 15" × 15" (38 cm × 38 cm). Photo: Keith Tidball

"Coffee Pot and Fish" (paper collage), 1989, 26" × 22" (65 cm × 56 cm). Photo: Keith Tidball

Flower Pot, 1987, 50" × 50" (127 cm × 127 cm). Photo: John Coles, Cornwall

"Sweetlips" (collage), 1989, 15" × 15" (38 cm × 38 cm). Photo: Keith Tidball

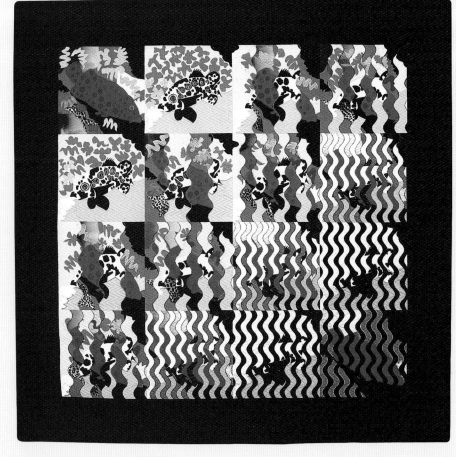

Joining Forces II, 1991, 78" × 76" (198 cm × 193 cm). Photo: Keith Tidball

"Coral Trout" (collage), 1989, 15" × 15" (38 cm × 38 cm). Photo: Keith Tidball

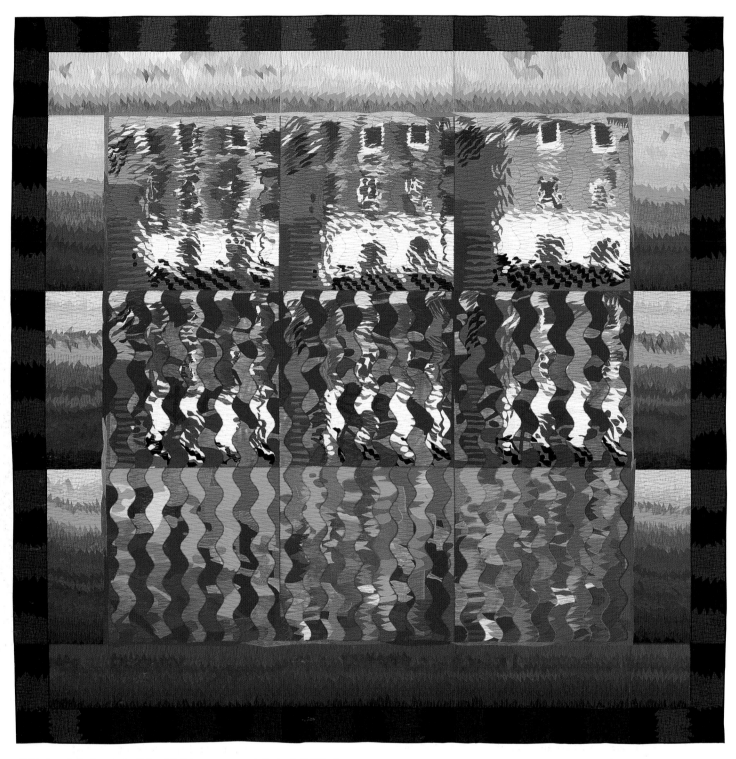

Nottingham Reflections, 1994, 82″ × 82″ (205 cm × 205 cm). Photo: Keith Tidball

Works in Progress: Further Techniques

CHAPTER 10

In this Workshop, I will share with you my own experiences and design decisions as two of my quilts developed. The Workshop covers two of my favorite techniques, which I am still developing. They are free-form fabric collage and laminating. First, I explain each technique through a simple hands-on project. I then show examples of finished quilts, describing the inspiration and the technical processes behind each one. I end each section by taking you step-by-step through the making of two quilts: *Dancing Lines*, a free-form collage quilt; and *Colourbank*, in which I used lamination. Tracing the growth of the whole work—from inspiration to finished quilt—will, I hope, provide helpful insight into how large-scale quilts develop.

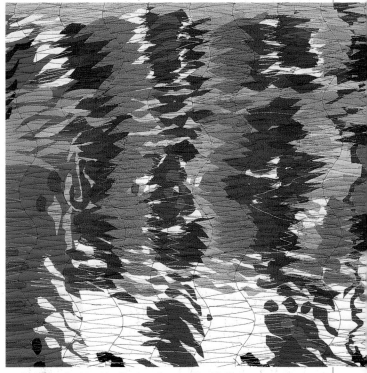

Nottingham Reflections (detail), 1994. Photo: Keith Tidball

WORKSHOP SUPPLIES

- General drawing equipment, including drawing board or surface 20″ × 20″ (50 cm × 50 cm)
- General sewing equipment, including sewing machine
- Fabric and paper scissors
- Masking tape
- 1 to 2 yds (1 to 2 m) fusible web, such as Bondaweb or Wonder-Under

- 1 yd (1 m) 100-percent-plain-white cotton for base cloth
- Selection of 100-percent-cotton fabrics in solid or plain colors
- Selection of machine threads and thicker hand-stitching threads
- Selection of photographs or magazine clippings (look for images with textural quality)

- Iron and ironing board
- Laminating plastic, such as Heat 'n Bond Vinyl
- Collection of loose threads or small fabric cuttings; other flat, dry, pliable items for laminating

Fish Out of Water (detail), 1991. Photo: Keith Tidball

Project 31 | **Free-Form Fabric Collage**

I have made several quilts using this technique. I usually begin by taking a few photographs, which I pin to the wall. Then I take a few pairs of scissors and a selection of fabrics prepared with fusible web. I begin cutting fabric shapes to create the images I see in the photographs. When a project goes well, I find this technique extremely liberating.

In the previous chapter we experimented with still-life images as a starting point for fabric collage, cutting out precise shapes that could be repeated. This project takes a freeer approach to design, creating the images as you cut the fabric. While this technique needs few tools, it does require confidence in handling fabric and color. *Fish Out of Water* uses simple, bold, free-form shapes. *Nottingham Reflections* on page 108 uses the same technique, but in that quilt there are many more layers of thin slices of fabric that make up the image.

1. Pin a selection of photographs to your design wall and choose one from which to work. Look for images that have a textile-like quality or that relate to fabric in some way. Choose clear, bold shapes of any image that you can easily envision made up in fabric and that reflect a theme that interests you.

2. Decide on the proportions and shape of your block and make sure they are appropriate to your source photograph. This may mean masking off an area of the image, i.e., masking part of a rectangular photo to make a square block.

3. Decide the size of your block and cut out a base block from solid white fabric. Add ½" (1.5 cm) seam allowances around all edges. For example, for a finished 12" (30 cm) block, you will need to cut the base fabric 13" (33 cm) square. Tape the base fabric to your drawing board.

Canal Reflections, 1993. Photo: Pauline Burbidge

Water pool detail, 1993. Photo: Pauline Burbidge

I used several different techniques in developing *Nottingham Reflections*, shown on page 108. The image is created through free-form collage (see Project 31). Some of the blocks are made though intercutting (see page 94). I have used satin stitch, zigzag, and free-motion stitching on the top fabric and free-motion stitching for the quilting. The work was quilted in three sections to make it easier to handle under the sewing machine. The sections were then joined together to complete the work.

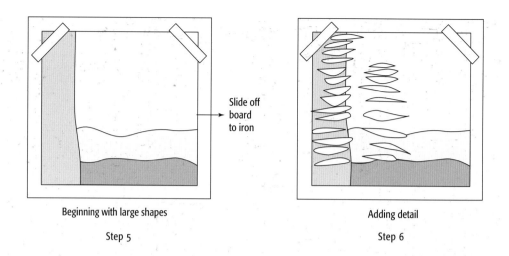

Slide off board to iron

Beginning with large shapes

Step 5

Adding detail

Step 6

- If one of your shapes does not work out well, simply position others right on top of it. This free-form technique allows for trial and error.
- You can build several layers of fabric collage, allowing the bottom layers to peek through the upper layers. Remember, though, that with more than four layers, the block becomes very thick and almost impossible to quilt.
- As an alternative approach, try a large-scale, rather than a block design. Keep in mind that if your finished piece is more than 2 yds (2 m) square, you will probably need to quilt it by hand rather than by machine.

4. Study the photographic image and select fabrics in the appropriate color range. Iron fusible web to the back of each of your selected fabrics. This is your color palette.

5. Look at the photograph again, this time dividing it into general areas of color. Choose the largest color area first and, using fabric scissors, cut freehand a piece of the matching fabric. Peel off the backing paper and position the fabric onto the base block. Cut the other larger areas also and position them in place. Then slide the entire block off the drawing board to iron. Return the block to the drawing board.

6. Cut out the finer, detailed shapes. Peel off the backing papers as you go and position them on the base cloth. When several are in position, remove the block from the drawing board and iron them on. Continue until the design is complete.

7. Pin the finished block to the design wall. Study it to assess how well the design works before moving on to the next block.

8. When all blocks are assembled, plus any border pieces that complete the quilt top, position them in place on the design wall. Choose stitches for the top fabric (see pages 17 and 18 for options), join blocks into appropriate sections, and quilt (see Chapter 3 for this).

NOTTINGHAM REFLECTIONS

I was offered a commission to create a piece based on the subject of water. Having completed quilts like *Intercut Fish—Harmony* (see page 86) on a similar theme, I jumped at the opportunity.

I began by taking photographs of water reflections along the canal banks in Nottingham. I very much enjoy taking photographs. I particularly like the fact that I can mask off my surroundings and concentrate on viewing details through the lens. I find that close-up photographs lend themselves beautifully for use as inspiration for abstract quilts. I came up with some very exciting images, but decided on this photo of a warehouse reflected in water. I loved the way the image of the building was broken up. I also found the proportions and the colors pleasing. Later, as I established the quilt image, I worked from a second photograph—a detail of a pool of water lined with blue tiles. I intercut this with the first image to create the six lower blocks.

On the River Tweed by
the Chain Bridge, 1995.
Photo: Pauline Burbidge

TWEED REFLECTIONS— FREE-FORM FABRIC COLLAGE

This quilt began from a series of photographs I took at the Chain Bridge by the River Tweed, a wonderful stretch of water near our home in the Scottish Borders. There was a beautiful stillness in the air as the water image slid through my vision in the camera lens. I wanted to try to capture some of this feeling in the quilt. The image I chose seemed to me to have a quality that was like strips of fabric, so I could immediately relate it to the materials with which I work.

The techniques I used were very similar to those used in *Dancing Lines*, described next. I stitched and quilted the separate blocks before assembling the whole quilt.

Tweed Reflections II (detail). Full quilt shown on page iii. Photo: Keith Tidball

WORK IN PROGRESS—*DANCING LINES*

For *Dancing Lines*, I collected images from two locales in the Scottish Borders—the river edge at Berwick-upon-Tweed and the Whiteadder Reservoir (see page 69). At the

reservoir, I was intrigued by reflections of a telegraph pole, which danced and moved as I shot the photographs. Hence, the quilt title. Unusual for me, here I worked from three separate images. The black, white, and gray areas of the quilt relate closely to the colors I observed in the waters; the deep, richer blues do not. These are my own personal color choices—colors that are close to my heart.

The techniques I used included free-form collage. I used satin stitch and zigzag stitch on the top fabric and straight stitching for the quilting. The photos that follow give you a clear picture of exactly how the work developed. From start to finish, it seemed to grow and flow naturally, without the stopping and rethinking that has been the more painful process of some of the quilts I have made.

Whiteadder Reservoir. Photo: Pauline Burbidge

Dancing Lines (detail). Full quilt shown on page 117. Photo: Keith Tidball

Preparing the fabric with fusible web (detail)

Preparing the fabric with fusible web

Cutting the collage shapes (detail)

Cutting the collage shapes. The backing paper is then peeled off and
shapes are assembled and ironed onto the base fabric.

Assembling
blocks on the
design wall

Stitching the top
cloth–free motion

Stitching the top cloth–free motion (detail)

Dancing Lines, 1998, 80" × 80" (203 cm
× 203 cm). Collection of the National
Museums of Scotland. Photo: Keith Tidball

Straight stitching as quilting (detail)

Back

Straight stitching as quilting

Front: joining the quilted blocks. Ironing on preglued fabric strips

Joining the blocks using free-motion quilting (detail)

Joining the blocks using free-motion quilting

Project 32 | **Laminating**

Laminating as a technique is rarely used in quiltmaking. A variety of materials, such as pressed leaves, petals, buttons, feathers, threads, grasses, fabric swatches, paper stamps, and any other small flat objects, are encased between a fabric and a laminating plastic, bonding to form a new fabric of sorts.

This project will take you through the technique I use to laminate fabric, producing a single block. Think of experimenting with this idea. You might increase the scale to a full-size quilt, or laminate a variety of different materials onto your fabric.

1. Cut out an 8" (20 cm) square of fabric and a 4" (10 cm) square of fusible web, such as Bondaweb or Wonder-Under. Iron the web onto the center of the right side of the fabric and peel off the backing paper, revealing the square of dry fabric glue beneath it.
2. Scatter a selection of loose threads over the dry glue and arrange them as desired.
3. Check the instructions for use on your laminating plastic, then cut a 6" (15 cm) square and peel off its backing paper. Smooth the plastic into position over the threads and the center square. It is slightly sticky and will cling to the fabric.

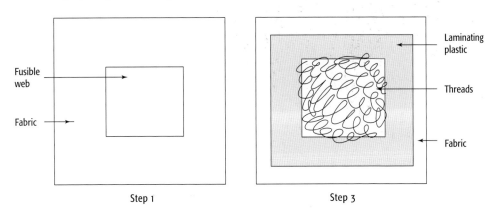

Step 1

Step 3

4. Turn the block over and press from the back with a medium-to-hot iron. Press quickly and lightly for about four to six seconds, bonding the plastic to the fabric. (If the plastic is overheated, it will blister.) Allow to cool for a few seconds before handling. Then place a little weight on it (you might use a book, for example); leave until it is completely cooled. This will stop it from curling up. The threads are now permanently trapped between the fabric and the plastic, bonding into a new piece of cloth that is ready for stitching into a quilt.
5. Try several more blocks, experimenting with your collected materials.

WORK IN PROGRESS—*COLOURBANK*

I produced a great deal of preliminary work before finally making this large laminated piece. Over a two-year period, I tested out the color and fastness of many petals and leaves. I made several smaller studies, including *Colour Study I*, shown on page 64. Since this piece came out so well, I was determined to make a large-scale quilt using many of the same plant species in a variety of color tones.

For *Colourbank*, I wanted the color to come from the petals, so I deliberately chose a similarly colored fabric onto which to laminate them. I hoped the viewer would first see the simple color blocks from a distance. Moving closer, the viewer would discover that the petals make up the color. The sheer difficulty of manipulating such a large-scale work, made more troublesome still by the plastic lamination, was daunting.

I began experimenting with lamination when making *Whiteadder* (see page 50). I wanted to lay down fabric strips in a very free-form way, throwing them onto the surface of the base fabric. I found I could not adequately stitch them in place, so I tried encasing them in plastic film over which I ran some machine stitching. I liked the results and began experimenting. I collected all kinds of flat objects and materials—threads, grasses, stamps, even tiny toys—and laminated them onto quilt block samples.

An interesting by-product was that my experiments really got me thinking about color. For a whole year, I collected objects—leaves, petals, and natural materials—from my garden and the surrounding countryside. I worked through the seasons, basically collecting colors. Without being aware of it, I was observing and recording color that was all around me. The experience heightened my color sensitivity, enriching my use of color in other fabric pieces.

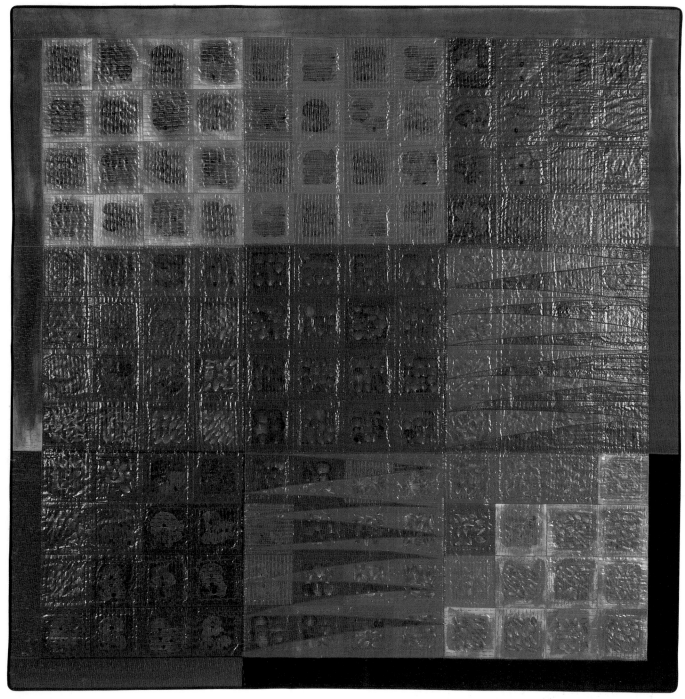

Colourbank, 1998, 78" × 78" (198 cm × 198 cm). Photo: Keith Tidball

Colourbank (detail). Photo: Keith Tidball

Laminating the blocks

Laminating the blocks (detail)

Assembling the blocks (detail)

Assembling the blocks

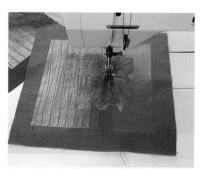

Stitching the blocks (detail)

Stitching the blocks

Joining the blocks to make the quilt top
(detail)

Joining the blocks to make the quilt top.
Note the strips of fabric backed with fusible web—used to join the blocks
on the back—are in the foreground of the photograph.

Large hand quilting stitches (detail)

Hand quilting with large stitches as the quilt is stretched over a frame

The only way in which I was able to quilt it was by hand in a frame. As you look at the images that show the work in progress, think of how you can begin with samples like my color studies and turn them into a finished large-scale quilt.

This Workshop concludes the projects in the book and brings you up to date on the types of ideas and processes I am using in the quilts I am currently working on. With each day and with each sample I work on, I try to discover something new that will help me express my experiences and my observations through my quilts. It is my hope that the projects and experiments I have shared with you here will encourage you to pursue new experiments and new ideas of your own.

Studio Quilts

TONE AND *BLACK AND WHITE FEATHERS*— LAMINATING

Tone, shown here and on page xviii, and *Black and White Feathers* were among the first pieces I made in my laminating series. I had spent several months collecting appropriate materials to laminate and finally settled on feathers. It seemed important to keep the black and white study simple, revealing the pure blackness and whiteness of those feathers. I took time to choose the gray fabrics for *Tone* since I wanted to achieve a good balance between the blocks.

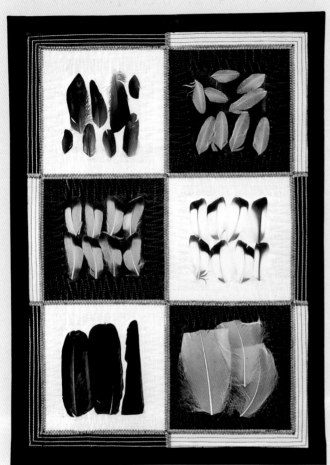

Black and White Feathers, 1996, 15" × 21" (38 cm × 53 cm). Photo: Keith Tidball

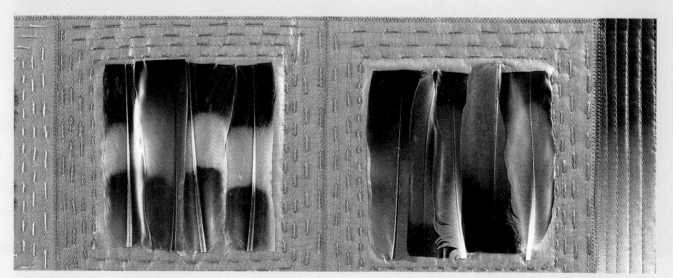

Tone (detail). Full quilt on page 126.
Photo: Keith Tidball

Tone, 1996, 27″ × 27″ (69 cm × 69 cm). Photo: Keith Tidball

Afterword: Beyond the Workshops

Once you have experimented with the various projects in *Quilt Studio*, you will be ready to develop your own ideas to their fullest. Every quilt begins with an impression of the finished work, whether you are conscious of that vision or not. A technique I find extremely helpful in working that vision toward a reality is to surround myself with the colors, images, and shapes that make up that early feeling of how the quilt will evolve. By collecting these together—on a design wall or on your work table—you can begin a visual dialogue with yourself. This will allow the quilt to develop naturally, from early conception to finished work.

Having said this, my next piece of advice is to keep your options open. Try not to be too set on making the quilt exactly how you first envisioned it. Changes take place as you work on a design concept. I have found that the quilts that please me the most are those where I allowed the work to develop naturally, changing course as it evolved. If you stick too rigidly to your original ideas, the work is static and will inevitably disappoint you when it is complete.

VISUAL LANGUAGE

Visual language is the key that makes your quilts different than those of any other quiltmaker. To explain what visual language is and how you can develop a visual language of your own, I would like to share with you my own discoveries. There may be some aspects of my experiences that you relate to strongly and others with which you entirely disagree. But by understanding how my visual language has evolved, it is my hope that you will get more closely in touch with your own ideas, preferences, and inspirations.

I am at my most creative when I do not have a rigid, preconceived concept for a finished quilt. It is easy to slip into a frame of mind where I take the work too seriously and I am too careful about keeping to the original plan. When that happens, the project begins to go badly and I have to start again. I remind myself to be prepared to make mistakes. This is difficult advice to follow. I need to relax yet at the same time be fully attentive. It is in this state that I find I can respond honestly to color and form. It is as though I enter a world that is purely connected to reaction—my work itself, in its purest form, is a reaction to the inspirations I have surrounded myself with.

Of course, not all my studio time has this quality. Much of my time is spent building up to these high points. I need to immerse myself in colors and shapes. I spend a great deal of time creating a connection with the world around me. I observe details in my surroundings—the countryside, the flora and fauna, plant forms, and the changing seasons. All this helps me feel that my work is emotionally connected to the celebration of life.

I find this sense of connection easier to explain by showing you my quilts. An ongoing project in recent years is a series of quilts that arose from my observations of reflections in water. I am fascinated with the ways water moves and dances, changing from one moment to the next. A clear image of a tree reflects in calm water; a moment later the wind blows and the entire image is broken up. In *Tweed Reflections II* (see page 32), nine blocks make up the image, giving the appearance of a traditional block quilt. Yet I really see those blocks as nine separate studies that record how images change as they are reflected in water. Water reflections continue to intrigue me, and I know I will explore this theme in my work for the foreseeable future.

Nature is a wonderful source, but your inspiration may be very different. Many quilters, for example, base their work on political ideas that are important to them. Others use quilts to explore deep emotional events in their lives; they cannot help but produce their work around these experiences. Our lives and our creativity are one.

Try not to expect to make your most expressive quilts right away. I suspect that many first-time quilters are disappointed if they are not able to produce top-quality exhibition work immediately. I certainly want to encourage quality work, but keep in mind that this takes a good deal of time, thought, and energy. If you are like most quiltmakers, your early work is likely to swing from one theme to the next, as you experiment and try out new ways of working. It is usually not a lack of ideas that keeps you from developing your own style but rather lack of concentration or patience to stick with and develop a theme. It's easy to allow yourself to be distracted and change course instead of exploring your original theme in more depth. The experience you gain from making one quilt leads very naturally into the next, and this is how you will develop a visual language of your own. Even if, early on, you make quilts that do not look like a "series," you can be sure there are visual links between them and, in time, if you persist, those links will become more and more apparent in your work.

In writing *Quilt Studio*, I have enjoyed sharing with you my technical expertise—learned through trial and error—and my own personal development as a quiltmaker. The writing has helped me as an artist as I have been forced to look closely at my work and the inspirations behind it. My greatest wish when I set out, however, was to help *you* develop as a quiltmaker. If this book inspires you, then I have achieved my goal.

Acknowledgments

A special thank you to those who have supported me and my work over the years. Your support has made it possible for me to continue working.

The Crafts Council; the Scottish Arts Council (Crafts Department); East Midlands Arts; the Shipley Art Gallery; the Whitworth Art Gallery; Nottingham Castle Museum; the Museum of Costume & Textiles–Nottingham; the Textile Museum–Washington DC; the National Museums of Scotland; the Ulster Folk and Transport Museum; the Glasgow Museums; the Victoria & Albert Museum; the Aberdeen Art Gallery; the Ruskin Craft Gallery; the Works Gallery; the Dairy Barn–Ohio; Foyles Art Gallery; the Angel Row; the Guild of St. George; the Embroiderers' Guild; the Quilters' Guild of the British Isles; the Association of Applied Arts; AXIS; Paintings in Hospitals Scotland; the Benjamin Britten High School; Artstream.

Michele Walker; Penny McMorris; Keith Tidball; John Coles; Michael James; Nancy Crow; Jan Myers-Newberry; Ardis and Robert James; John M. Walsh; Roberta Kniestedt; Ron Simpson; Naomi Ichikawa; Jenny and Alec Hutchison; Angela Chisholm; Hazel Mills; Diana Springall; Dorothy Osler; Matthew Koumis; June Freeman; Lynne Edwards; Inge Heuber; Isabel Dibden-Wright; Anne Morrell; Ann Sutton; Kate and Wallace Anderson; Christine Rew; Alison Wilson; Janet Rae; Mary Fogg; Jenny Hollingdale; Sir Gerald and Lady Margaret Elliot; Shiela Betterton; Andrew James; Adam Lury and Claire Crocker; Helen Bennett; Liz Arthur; Michaela Butter; Jeremy Farrell; Helen Joseph; Naomi Tarrant; Vanessa and Gareth Morris; Rebecca and Gary Stevens; Jennifer Harris; Linda Theophilus; Matilda Mitchell and Douglas Hall; Katharine Gurrier; Maria Koval and Tony Saggers; Jim Nelson and Sue Bailey; Rita Alker; Lyn Wigfield; Jane Barff; Jane Campbell; Iona and David Heath; Erica Hörr; Jon and Jeanette Purday; John Papper; Pamela Martin and Peter Chatwin; Kate Houghton and Pete Wyatt; Andrew Budden; Hilary Fletcher; Juddith Duffey-Harding; Louise Butler; Helen Douglas and Telfer Stokes; Anitra Rushbrook and David Sinclair; Len and Jean McDermid; Eiluned Edwards; Erica Just; Julia Fenby; Moira Vincentelli; Celia Eddy; Averil Clavey; Cherry Vernon-Harcourt; Janet Pilkington; Maddi Nicholson and Stuart Bastik; Jo Budd; Dinah Prentice; Nancy and Walter Herman; Patty Hawkins; James Kingston-Stewart; Dean Neuman; Dierdre Amsden; Joen (Zinni) Goodman; Yvonne Porcella; Michael Kile; Barry Prothero; Molly and Robin Evans; Hanna Klein; Sandra Shikuma; Janis Ito; Meg Small; Penny and Philip

Credits

Photography by Keith Tidball, Nottingham, U.K., with the following exceptions:

- Photography, as credited on page by John Coles, Cornwall, U.K. (Tel: 01566-774507; E-mail: kersound@globalnet.co.uk)
- Miscellaneous photographs of landscape details are by Pauline Burbidge.
- *Allanbank Caravan* by Michael James on page 53 was photographed by David Caras.

    All textile works and paper collages are by Pauline Burbidge, except *Allanbank Caravan* by Michael James on page 53.

    For the quilts *Joining Forces* and *Joining Forces II* and the paper collage "Coral Trout," I worked from a photograph by Leni Riefenstahl from her book *Coral Gardens*.

    All sculpture shown is by Charles Poulsen.

Roberts; Pat Jonas; Angelo Chinque; Alyne Hamilton; John and Marion Pryor; John and Wendy Walker.

Thank you also to Anne Knudsen and everyone at The Quilt Digest Press for publishing my book.

A special thanks to my mum and the Burbidges, and to my husband, Charlie, and the Poulsens.

Bibliography

Work of Pauline Burbidge in Other Publications

Barker, Vicki and Tessa Bird, *The Fine Art of Quilting*, Studio Vista, London, 1990

Burbidge, Pauline, *Making Patchwork for Pleasure and Profit*, John Gifford Ltd., London, 1981

Lintott, Pam and Rosemary Miller, *The Quilt Room*, Charles Letts, London, 1992

Nihon Vogue (ed), *88 Leaders in the Quilt World Today*, Nihon Vogue, Tokyo, 1994

Shaw, Robert, *Quilts—A Living Tradition*, Hugh Lauter Levin Associates, 1995

———, *The Art Quilt*, Hugh Lauter Levin Associates, 1997

Walker, Michele, *Quiltmaking in Patchwork and Appliqué*, Ebury Press, London, 1985

———, *The Passionate Quilter*, Ebury Press, London, 1990

Work of Pauline Burbidge in Selected Catalogs

Butter, Michaela, *Quilt Art*, Nottingham Castle Museum, Nottingham, 1988

Harris, Jennifer, *Take 4—New Perspectives on the British Art Quilt*, The Whitworth Art Gallery and Telos Art Publishing, Manchester, 1998

McMorris, Penny and Michael Kile, *The Art Quilt*, The Quilt Digest Press, Lincolnwood, IL, 1996

Segawa, Setsuki, *New Wave Quilt Collections II*, Mitsumura Suika Shoin, Kyoto, 1992

Profiles

Crow, Nancy, *Nancy Crow, Quilts & Influences*, American Quilters Society, Paducah, KY, 1990

James, Michael, *Michael James Studio Quilts*, Whetstone Hill Publications, Swansea, MA, 1995

———, *Art & Inspirations*, C&T Publishing, Martinez, CA, 1998

Textiles

Askari, Nasreen and Rosemary Crill, *Colours of the Indus: Costume and Textiles of Pakistan*, Merrell Holberton, London, 1997

Desai, Chelna, *Ikat Textiles of India*, Thames Hudson, London, 1989

Harris, Jennifer, *5000 Years of Textiles*, British Museum Press, London, 1993

Koumis, Matthew, *Art Textiles of the World: Great Britain*, Telos Art Publishing, Winchester, MA, 1996

———, *Art Textiles of the World: Japan*, Telos Art Publishing, Winchester, MA, 1997

———, *Art Textiles of the World: USA*, Telos Art Publishing, Winchester, MA, 2000

Picton, John and John Mack, *African Textiles*, British Museum Publications, London, 1989

The Rau Collection (ed), *Ikats: Woven Silk from Central Asia*, Basil Blackwell with The Crafts Council, Oxford, 1988

Quilting

Osler, Dorothy, *Quilting*, Merehurst, London, 1991

Color

Guild, Tricia and Elizabeth Wilhide, *Tricia Guild on Color*, Conran Octopus, London, 1992

Itten, Johannes, *Itten: The Elements of Color*, Van Nostrand Reinhold, Co., New York, 1970

Mella, Dorothee L., *The Language of Color*, Penguin Books, London, 1990

Zelanski, Paul and Mary Pat Fisher, *Color*, The Herbert Press, London, 1989

Pattern

Bain, George, *Celtic Art*, Stuart Titles, Glasgow, 1990

Bezuska, Stanley, Margaret Kenney, and Linda Silvey, *Tessellations: The Geometry of Patterns*, Creative Publications, Montain View, CA, 1977

Blossfeldt, Karl, *Art Forms in the Plant World*, Dover Publications, New York, 1929 and 1985

————, *Natural Art Forms*, Dover Publications, New York, 1932 and 1998

Bourgoin, Jules, *Arabic Geometrical Pattern and Design*, Dover Publications, New York, 1973

Courtney-Clarke, Margaret, *African Canvas*, Rizzoli International Publications, Inc., New York, 1990

Feininger, Andreas, *Shells, Forms, and Designs of the Sea*, Dover Publications, New York, 1983

Field, Robert, *Geometric Patterns from Tiles and Brickwork*, Tarquin Publications, Diss, Norfolk (U.K.), 1996

Gerster, Georg, *Flights of Discovery: The Earth from Above*, Paddington Press, London, 1978

Jones, Owen, *The Grammar of Ornament*, Bernard Quaritch, 1910

Joseph, Michael, *Decorative Endpapers: The Victoria & Albert Colour Book*, Webb & Bower, London, 1985

Oliver, June, *Polysymetrics: The Art of Making Geometric Patterns*, Tarquin Publications, Diss, Norfolk (U.K.), 1979

Phillips, Peter and Gillian Bunce, *Repeat Patterns*, Thames and Hudson, London, 1993

Proctor, Richard, *The Principles of Pattern Design*, Dover Publications, New York, 1990

Wiltshire, Alan, *Three Dimensions and Impossible Solids*, Claire Publications, Colchester, Essex (U.K.), 1992

Fabric Dyeing and Painting

Adrosko, Rita J., *Natural Dyes and Home Dyeing*, Dover Publications, New York, 1971

Campbell-Harding, Valerie, *Fabric Painting for Embroidery*, Batsford, London, 1990

Storey, Joyce, *The Thames & Hudson Manual of Dyes and Fabrics*, Thames & Hudson, London, 1992

Collage

Adler, Peter and Nicholas Barnard, *Asafo! African Flags of the Fante*, Thames & Hudson, London, 1992

Rodari, Florian, *Collage: Pasted, Cut, and Torn Papers*, Skira Rizzoli, New York, 1988

Works of Pauline Burbidge in Public Collections

United States

Finn, 1983, the Robert and Ardis James Collection, the International Quilt Study Center at the University of Nebraska, Lincoln, Nebraska

Eternal Triangle, 1983, the Robert and Ardis James Collection, the International Quilt Study Center at the University of Nebraska, Lincoln, Nebraska

The Pink Teapot, 1987, the Robert and Ardis James Collection, the International Quilt Study Center at the University of Nebraska, Lincoln, Nebraska

Spirals I, 1985, the Robert and Ardis James Collection, the International Quilt Study Center at the University of Nebraska, Lincoln, Nebraska

Spirals II, 1985, the Robert and Ardis James Collection, the International Quilt Study Center at the University of Nebraska, Lincoln, Nebraska

Nottingham Reflections, 1994, Collection of John M. Walsh III (This is a private collection, sometimes displayed in public galleries.)

Tweed Reflections II, 1995, Collection of John M. Walsh III (This is a private collection, sometimes displayed in public galleries.)

United Kingdom

Pyramid II, 1980, the Crafts Council, London

Floating Triangles, 1983, the Ruskin Gallery, Sheffield (Collection of the Guild of St. George)

Mirrored Steps, 1983, Shipley Art Gallery, Gateshead

Kate's Vase, 1987, the Victoria & Albert Museum (Textile Department)

The Pink Teapot, 1986 (paper collage), Art for Schools Collection, Sheffield Galleries and Museums Trust, Sheffield

Blue Fish, 1986 (fabric collage), Art for Schools Collection, Sheffield Galleries and Museums Trust, Sheffield

3 Fish & Stripe, 1991 (paper collage), Paintings in Hospitals Scotland (PIH), Edinburgh

Barrels, 1991 (paper collage), Paintings in Hospitals Scotland (PIH), Edinburgh

Matt & Bowl, 1991 (paper collage), Paintings in Hospitals Scotland (PIH), Edinburgh

Sweetlips II, 1989, Museum of Costume & Textiles, Nottingham

Joining Forces II, 1991, Museum of Costume & Textiles, Nottingham

Reflections, 1993, Museum of Costume & Textiles, Nottingham

Striped Canopy, 1990, the Old Library Theater Company and Arts Center, Mansfield

Canopy II, 1990, the Old Library Theater Company and Arts Center, Mansfield

Joining Forces, 1989, the Whitworth Art Gallery, Manchester

Custard Squash II, 1989, Ulster Folk and Transport Museum, Belfast

Intercut Fish—Harmony, 1992, Glasgow Museums, Glasgow
Dancing Lines, 1998, National Museums of Scotland, Edinburgh
Circular Series No. 5, 1984, the Embroiderers Guild Collection, London
Fishdance, 1991, the Quilters Guild of the British Isles, Halifax
Small Zig-Zag Quilt, 1991, the Quilters Guild of the British Isles, Halifax

Note: Please make sure you phone the museums to arrange to see the work before your visit.
It may not be on permanent display.

Sources and Supplies

Quilt stores are becoming increasingly diversified and more and more of them now carry specialized materials, such as fabric dyes and paints. If you are unable to find the equipment you need at local quilt and craft stores, these sources may help.

Magazines

Quilters Newsletter Magazine. Contains advertisements for specialty shops and suppliers of quiltmaking goods. PO Box 59021, Boulder, CO 80322

The Art Quilt Magazine. Contains advertisements for specialty shops and suppliers of quiltmaking goods. Dept S, PO Box 630927, Houston, TX 77263-0927.

The Quilter (U.K.). Magazine with advertisements for specialty shops and suppliers of quiltmaking goods. The Quilters Guild of the British Isles, Room 190, Dean Clough, Halifax, West Yorkshire, HX3 5AX. Tel: 01422-347-669.

Quilting Supplies and Fabrics

In the United States, most well-stocked quilt shops will carry everything you need. In the U.K., stores like these are a little harder to find. Here are a few sources I can recommend.

Strawberry Fayre (U.K.), Chagford, Devon, TQ13 8EN. Tel: 01647-433-250. Mail-order company specializing in fabrics.

The Quilt Room (U.K.), 20 West Street, Dorking, Surrey, RH4 1BL. Tel: 01306-740-739. Patchwork and quilting supply shop. Also their mail order company is: rear carvilles (The Quilt Room), Station Road, Dorking, Surrey, RH4 1XH. Tel: 01306-877-307.

Purely Patchwork (U.K.), 23 High Street, Linlithgow, W. Lothian, Scotland, EH49 7AB. Tel: 01506-846-200. Patchwork and quilting supply shop.

W.B.L. Whaleys (Bradford) Ltd. (U.K.), Harris Court, Great Horton, Bradford, West Yorkshire, BD7 4EQ. Tel: 01274-576-718. Specialist in basic fabrics suitable for quilting, dyeing, painting, and collage.

Laminating Plastic

W. Williams & Son Ltd. (U.K.), Regent House, 1 Thane Villas, London, N7 7PH. Tel: 0171-263-7311. Supplier of laminating plastic.

Therm O Web (U.S.), 770 Glenn Avenue, Wheeling, IL 60090. Tel: 847-520-5200. Supplier of laminating plastic.

Thread

Coats American. Head office (U.S.): Two Lakepointe Plaza, 4135 South Stream Blvd, Charlotte, NC 28217. Tel: 704-329-5800.

Coats & Clark (U.S.), Greenville, SC 29615. Tel: 800-243-0810. Call for a stock list of *coton à broder*.

Coats Craft (U.K.), Darlington, DL1 1YQ, Tel: 01325-394-394. Call for a stock list of *coton à broder*.

Coats Limited. Head office (U.K.): Desford Road Enderby, Leicester, LE9 5AS. Tel: 0116-275-2020.

I buy thread in large quantities. A bulk catalog is available from Coats. My favorite thread is Sylco #36.

Batting (Wadding)

The Warm Company (U.S.), 954 East Union Street, Seattle, WA 98122. Tel: 206-320-9276. There are many types of batting (or wadding) available. To find the ones that work best for you, buy small sample pieces of a few and try them out. The one I favor is Warm & Natural by The Warm Company. Call for a local stock list.

Fabric Dyes

Kemtex Educational Supplies (U.K.), Chorley Business & Technology Centre, Euxton Lane, Chorley, Lancashire, PR7 6TE. Tel: 01257-230-220. Suppliers of dyes and related chemicals.

Pro-Chemical & Dye, Inc., PO Box 14, Somerset, MA 02726. Tel: 508-676-3838.

Fabric Paints

Daler-Rowney Ltd. (U.K.), Bracknell, Berkshire, RG12 8ST. Tel: 01344-424-621. I use two types of acrylic fabric paint: Screen & Fabric printing color, a ready-mixed paint with a separate extender medium, and System 3 Textile Painting Medium, which mixes with acrylic paint. Contact for a stock list.

Daler-Rowney USA, (U.S.), 2 Corporate Drive, Cranbury, NJ 08512-9584. Tel: 609-655-5252. I use two types of acrylic fabric paint: Screen & Fabric printing color, a ready-mixed paint with a separate extender medium, and System 3 Textile Painting Medium, which mixes with acrylic paint. Contact for a stock list.

Glossary of Specialized Terms

To avoid confusion between American and British terminology for specialized quiltmaking materials, I hope this short glossary is helpful.

Calico: Plain woven, unbleached, undyed cotton fabric, available in several widths and in several weights (light, medium, and heavy). Medium-weight calico compares to thicker patchwork cotton fabrics. When new, calico has a stiff quality, which is the size dressing on the fabric. The dressing is not permanent and washes out in a hot wash, which then changes the quality to a soft medium-weight basic cotton fabric. I find calico ideal to use as the base cloth for fabric collage. Calico is a little heavier than the fabric known as muslin in the United States. In the United States, calico is understood to mean a printed fabric with a floral pattern.

Coton à broder: This is a great hand-sewing thread for large stitching. It is 100% cotton and comes in several thicknesses. No. 16 is a medium thickness. A stock list is available from Coats Limited and Coats & Clark, as listed under Sources and Supplies.

Fusible web: Iron-on or fabric glue, also known in the U.K. as transfer adhesive, is available from quiltmaking, sewing, and craft stores and from specialty mail-order companies as listed under Sources and Supplies. Major U.S. brands include Wonder-Under and Heat 'n Bond. Major U.K. brands include Bondaweb.

Muslin: Unbleached, medium-weight cotton fabric similar in quality to calico. (Do not confuse with the muslin available in the U.K.—a very loose weave fabric used for bandaging and for straining foods.)

Plain fabric: Single-color, non-patterned fabric (U.K.).

Plain white cotton: Plain-weave, medium-weight, bleached cotton. Ideal for dyeing or painting.

Solid fabric: Single-color, non-patterned fabric (U.S.).

Index